Jere

Cognitive Behavioral Therapy

The new 5-step system to
end anxiety, defuse anger,
defeat depression & negative
thinking, manage panic
attacks and phobias, improve
your social skills.

Contents

Introduction

While the term 'cognitive behavioral therapy' is largely unknown by the general population, among therapists, psychologists, and psychiatrists it is known to be a powerful tool in mental healing. But, while you may be unaware of the details the practice entails, you have most likely heard of some of the tools and processes it promotes and their benefits. In this book, you will learn about the details of cognitive behavioral therapy, known as CBT, and how it can aid you during your daily life. Whether you are struggling with the stresses of daily life, negative thought patterns, anger management difficulties, depression, anxiety, or a number of other mental illnesses, you can find healing with this method. You may be wondering what CBT entails. This method is based on the cognitive theory in the psychopathology field. Whether you are coping with daily stress and negative thought patterns or mental

illness, CBT can help as it is based on how these worries and stressors affect both a person's psyche and behaviors.
The cognitive model explains that many of our behaviors are based directly off of our emotions, which in turn influence our thought patterns and decision making. Whether your emotions are conscious or subconscious, they can lead you to make decisions that are either helpful or unhelpful. Thankfully, with cognitive behavioral therapy, you can learn to harness your emotions and decision making to help you choose healthier and more balanced decisions.

Over time, you will learn to replace negative, damaging, and false ideas and thought with healthier more realistic thoughts. CBT is able to do this by first helping you become aware of which thoughts are damaging, and then teaching you how to replace them with something more balanced. This form of therapy has been found to be one of the most effective types of psychotherapy, sometimes working as well as anti-anxiety and antidepressant drugs. Of course, this therapy can't always replace the use of medication, but it can greatly improve your mental health both alone and with the addition of medication if your doctor believes it is needed. No longer do you have to allow stress, anxiety, and anger to lead to distorted ideas and poor choices. You can learn to take control of your emotions and thoughts for a better mental state and life. Before long, you will find that you are happier and more in control, with the ability to make your life flourish.

Part One:

How to Practically Control the Most Important Emotions in 5 Easy Steps

Chapter 1: Consider Negativity a Red Flag

As humans we tend to trust in our own emotions thoughts, after all, these originate in our brain, and if we don't trust our own selves what else can we trust? In general, it's a good thing to be able to listen to your brain. We experience many conscious and unconscious thoughts throughout the day that help us to cope, excel, solve problems, and stay safe from danger.

But, our brains don't always tell us the truth. While it's important to listen to our inner thoughts and emotions, we must analyze these for truth and determine if they are safe to believe and act on. Your brain won't purposefully lie to you, but, due to developing incorrect negative thought processes overtime and mental illness we can become misleading. In fact, you would be surprised how easy it is for our brains to create these incorrect thought processes. As the human brain is predisposed to creating connections between our emotions, ideas, thoughts, actions, and consequences, it can begin to create connections even if the aspects it believes are connected are not.

You may be surprised by how easily the human brain can create faulty connections. This is the reason for the well-known saying "correlation does not equal causation," which is frequently used in the scientific community while researchers attempt to understand and interpret research and studies. But, this phrase is not just true in the scientific aspect, but on a fundamental mental level, as well. While it may be easy to believe that various coincidences and actions or results are somehow tied together, there are often deeper events that we are over-simplifying. These types of mistakes are a part of human nature, but one that we can largely overcome. In order to help people better understand this process of faulty connections and ideas, researchers have studied its effects extensively. This process is known as cognitive distortions and is often the cause of the negativity that humans struggle with. But, if you learn about your negativity and cognitive distortions you can learn how to turn your thinking around into something more balanced and healthy, helping to reveal the truth of situations to you while creating a healthier mental and emotional state.

A good example of cognitive distortions is one known as negative filtering, which is a type that we all struggle with on occasion. With this type of cognitive distortion, we will abandon thinking about any positive possibilities or aspects of a situation and instead, focus solely on the negative. We simply filter anything positive out of our thought processes and decision making, which leaves us with an abundance of negative thoughts.

A good example of negative filtering is when you usually get high grades on class assignments, but if you get one lower grade, you might immediately begin to believe that you are "incompetent," "stupid," or a "failure." Alternatively, if you have a deadline for work coming up you might begin to feel stressed and think that you will miss the deadline and get fired. You think negatively rather than keeping in mind that you are on schedule and unlikely to get fired even if you were a little late.

There are many sources of negative thinking and filtering. You will often find that in your daily life this form of cognitive dysfunction is caused by having unrealistically high expectations of yourself or others. This can present itself as you believing that something always has to be done perfectly; there can be no mistakes or unexpected events. You judge everything that you do or that occurs around you against an unattainable sense of perfection. When a person does manage to achieve seeming perfection, it is simply what is expected, and they don't see the accomplishment for what it is. On the other hand, if they fail to meet these ideas of perfection, then they are a failure and all past success of null and void. All that matters is that in this instance the person was unable to measure up to their ideal of perfection.

It is plain to see how negative filtering can cause great harm to a person, especially over time as it becomes a habit. This damaging thought process causes a person to think of only the negative, pounding away at a person's self-esteem, decreasing their mood, increasing their anxiety, and possibly leading to depression. A person gets stuck in a cycle of negative thoughts and pessimism, making it more difficult to have positive thoughts the longer this cycle goes on. Mental health professionals have found that negative filtering is the most common type of cognitive distortion for people struggling with depression. Therefore, in the treatment of depression, it is vital to find and target these negative thoughts in order to overturn them and led a person to a more balanced truth where they can once again see the positive.

When you struggle with negative filtering, it is important that you learn to recognize when you may be participating in this line of thinking. It is important to recognize when you are thinking negatively so that you can then stop and examine the actual evidence of a situation and search for the truth. Whether you are struggling with thoughts of yourself or a situation that you find yourself in, stop and look for anything that isn't completely bad. Look for any positives in the situation or anything that you can be grateful for. Is everything really all bad, or are there various degrees of good and bad in the situation? Would other people you know come to the same conclusion of negativity as you have and if they wouldn't what are they focusing on that you are missing?

Consider the opposite of what your negative thoughts are telling you. For instance, consider that you will be able to make a deadline, that you won't get fired, or that you aren't a failure. While considering the opposite scenario, analyze if there is more evidence that supports this more positive and balanced thought process. By analyzing the situation and considering positives rather than taking negative filtering at face value you can learn to look at things in a more balanced and rational manner. You will be less dependent on your negative moods or depression and able to learn to cope with negative thoughts. When you struggle with negative filtering, it is vital that you stay ever vigilant so that you can overcome your pessimistic thought cycles. You have the ability to change the way you think, examine your thoughts, and increase your mood. It may take some time to overcome this vicious cycle, but you will find that it gets easier as you adjust to a more balanced way of thinking.

To summarize what you have learned, cognitive

distortions are biases and incorrect ideas we adopt about ourselves and the world as a whole. We unconsciously reinforce these irrational beliefs and ideas over time, until they become a habit and second-nature. You may not notice these illogical thought patterns when they first arise, as they are subtle and can hide in your regular day-to-day thoughts.

Yet, they are damaging in this way because we often don't even know that we are dealing with cognitive distortions; therefore they are allowed to spread and take over until we are overcome with distortions. There are many types of cognitive distortions, such as negative filtering, but they share certain common factors. These include patterns of ideas or thinking that are inaccurate or false and have the potential to cause emotional and mental pain and damage. David Burns, a renowned psychiatrist who is an expert in the field of cognitive behavioral therapy and cognitive distortions once said:

"I suspect you will find that a great many of your negative feelings are in fact based on such thinking errors." It is easy to ignore your cognitive distortion. In fact, we want to ignore the idea that our thinking may be distorted, as it is scary to admit. You want to believe that your thinking is clear, reasonable, and true. You don't want to believe that you are holding onto false ideas and beliefs. But, in order to overcome cognitive dysfunction and negative ideas, we must learn to see these cognitive distortions for what they are and learn to search for the truth. We can encounter these distortions on a daily basis, which means you always have a chance to improve and work on developing a habit of seeking true and balanced beliefs.

If you are someone who struggles with cognitive distortions on a regular and day-to-day basis, then it will take time to overcome these ideas. Don't be discouraged if other people are able to overcome their distortions more quickly. We are each individuals and learn things at different paces. This is especially true with cognitive dysfunctions when people struggle with different types of distortions and experience them at different frequencies. While one person may only struggle with cognitive distortions a few times a week, another person may live struggling with these distortions on a near-constant basis. Of course, it will take the person who lives with these distortions longer to overcome them than a person who only struggles with them occasionally. That's okay. The road to healing and cognitive balance is not a race.

These cognitive distortions are especially difficult to overcome when they are paired with clinical depression. This is because the two often go hand-in-hand, and cognitive distortions and negative ideas excel at exacerbating and increasing the painful symptoms of depression. Cognitive distortions do not necessarily cause depression, but they frequently occur together, and it is well-documented how these false perceptions can worsen a person's mental health.

When studying cognitive distortions, you will often hear the names of the previously mentioned David Burns, as well as Aaron Beck. Burns and Beck, both psychiatrists, literally wrote the book(s) on cognitive distortions and their role on depression, anxiety, other mental health conditions, and the required treatment protocols with a form of early cognitive behavioral therapy.

Dr. David Burns studied and graduated from the Stanford University of Medicine before later going on to study further at the University of Pennsylvania School of Medicine. Once he graduated from the Pennsylvania university, Dr. Burns completed his psychiatry residency.

Dr. Burns continues to help the following generations learn about mental illness and cognitive distortions while serving as a professor emeritus of psychiatry and behavioral sciences at his alma mater, Stanford University School of Medicine. Along with serving as professor emeritus, Dr. Burns continues to research into depression and psychotherapy while teaching future therapists how to help their patients better. Many of Dr. Burn's theories on psychotherapy deal with cognitive distortions and how they impact mental health, and therefore the importance of correcting these false distortions.

Dr. Aaron Beck, the other leader in the field of cognitive distortions, graduated from Yale Medical School, where he continued to serve his psychiatry residency. During this time he became passionate about the research and treatment of depression and suicide. This lead Dr. Beck to join the University of Pennsylvania's Department of Psychiatry, where he is the professor emeritus of psychiatry.

Dr. Beck founded the well-renowned Beck Initiative, in order to teach future therapists how to utilize cognitive behavioral therapy in order to help their patients overcome cognitive distortions. The Beck Initiative has helped to greatly further CBT to become the well-known and powerful form of therapy it is today.

Along with creating the Beck Initiative, Dr. Beck published a multitude of books and other publications in order to research and further the knowledge of this form of psychotherapy. Joining the National Institute of Mental Health, he has even served as an editor to aid in the release of peer-reviewed journals. On occasion, Dr. Beck will visit various universities and other academic institutions worldwide in order to share his knowledge.

While Dr. Beck is well-renowned for many achievements, awards, and degrees, the largest impact he has made is in the creation of cognitive behavioral therapy. Dr. Beck is the doctor who noticed that many people who struggle with depression also struggle with cognitive distortions and false ideas. His hypothesis that by changing a patient's thinking and cognition that he could help treat and manage the depression proved true, leading to the powerful psychotherapy we know today.

Now that you have an understanding of cognitive distortions and the doctors who came to understand and teach on these ideas. Let's look at a complete list of the types of cognitive distortions. There are many lists you can find out there, some helpful and others less helpful. But, this list contains the sixteen most common types of cognitive distortions as taught by Dr. Burns himself.

By learning to recognize these cognitive distortions and their negativity, you can learn to watch out for them in your daily life. Once you know what you are facing you can better be prepared and overcome the struggle.

1. **Polarized Thinking**

   This is also known as "all or nothing" and "black and white" thinking, as this type of cognitive distortion shows itself as a person having an extreme unwillingness or inability to see the shades of gray between the black and white. A person only sees circumstances in one of two extremes, and are unable or unwilling to see that it may be more balanced than they are accepting. A situation is not necessarily completely terrible, and you are not a total failure. Things can be difficult or frustrating without being completely black. It's important to learn to see the shades of gray both in life and in yourself.

2. **Overgeneralization**

With the overgeneralization distortion, a person can begin to believe that one or a few instances are indicative of an overall pattern. For instance, if a person fails to meet a deadline, gets angry during a stressful situation, receives a bad grade, or experiences a bad relationship they may begin to believe that something is wrong with them, rather than accepting that difficult situations are simply a part of life and will happen to everyone. One or two instances don't make a pattern and aren't an indication of what type of person you are or what you can expect in life.

3. Mental Filter

The mental filter distortion is similar to that of the overgeneralization one, as it causes a person to hyper-focus on a single negative thought and abandon all positive thoughts. For instance, a person may have handled a situation with a customer at their job poorly, and therefore believe that they are unfit for their job, that all their years of working there and training amount to nothing. They completely ignore the many positive experiences they have had with customers and the fact that they usually excel at their job. With the mental filter distortion, it is as if you are standing in a house of mirrors, which distort everything to look negative.

4. Disqualifying the Positives

Unlike the mental filter distortion, with the disqualifying the positives distortion a person is able to see and acknowledge positives within a situation. Yet, rather than embracing the positives they reject them. For instance, if a person receives positive feedback from their employer, teacher, parent, or partner they may completely reject the idea. People with this distortion believe that the praise is solely due to kindness, political correctness, or encouragement that isn't based in reality. They think that people who offer them praise are only being nice despite their perceived flaws. With this distortion, you are unable to accept the positives people say, as you hold a negative view of yourself and are unwilling to accept anything that contradicts this view. This type of cognitive distortion is especially damaging and difficult to overcome, as it attempts to remain despite the positives and evidence to the contrary.

5. **Jumping to Conclusions**

Also known as "mind reading," the jumping to conclusions distortion leads to a person assuming that they know what others are thinking and creating false and inaccurate ideas off of this belief. While we can certainly have an idea of what another person might be thinking, with this distortion a person has a habit of automatically jumping to the worse conclusion of interpretation. For instance, you might assume that everyone you talk to is annoyed by your presence, dislikes you, or upset about something you said.

6. **Fortune Telling**

Similar to the jumping to conclusions distortion, fortune telling is when a person has little evidence yet creates a prediction of a situation and holds it to be completely true. For instance, a person may be convinced that they will never be able to make friends or be in a committed relationship, simply because they have not had much success yet. But, there is no way to know that you will never have success in these areas, and holding onto the negative idea that you won't is self-sabotaging and damaging. There are many possible future outcomes, and it is important not to hold onto a single possibility as fact, especially when it is negative.

7. Catastrophizing and Minimizing

This type of cognitive distortion is also known as the "binocular trick" as people struggling with it have a skewed perception regarding the importance of situations. They either incorrectly enlarge or minimize the importance of themselves or whatever situation at hand they are experiencing. For instance, someone who is a new parent and makes a small mistake may enlarge the problem and imagine it as something terrible and unforgivable. Similarly, someone who wins an award at their job may minimize their success and continue to believe that they are only subpar.

8. Emotional Reasoning

One of the most important distortions to understand, identify, and address may hide from and surprise many people. This is because nearly every person has struggled with this type of cognitive distortion at one point or another. With the emotional reasoning distortion, a person doesn't only acknowledge their feelings; they accept their feelings as having a basis in truth and completely factual. For instance, a person may believe that because they feel someone dislikes them or because they feel something is right it must be true. It is easy at the moment to think that your feelings are telling you the truth, but we can't always accept everything they tell us. Instead of acting on your emotions at the moment, it is important to analyze them and see the truth behind them.

9. Should Statements

Another common and damaging distortion are should statements. This occurs when a person believes they or someone else "should" do or have done something. But, when creating these statements a person is often setting themselves a high standard that is difficult to meet, and if they are unable to meet this expectation, then they see themselves as a failure. On the other hand, when they make these statements against others, it can lead to resentment, anger, and the person believing that they are better than those who fail to meet up to their standard of "should have." For instance, a parent may feel like a failure because they believe they should breastfeed but instead must bottle feed due to unexpected circumstances. When it comes to other people, a parent may judge other parents as "selfish" or "less than" because they choose to bottle feed, use disposable diapers, or make other parenting decisions that the parent in question doesn't think should be made.

10. Labeling and Mislabeling

The labeling and mislabel distortion is like the overgeneralization distortion but taken to the extreme. Like with overgeneralization, a person will judge themselves and others based off of a single experience or instance. But, with this more extreme version, the distortion is highly emotional and often uses loaded language. For instance, a person who is unable to answer a trivia question or math problem may believe themselves to be "a complete and utter idiot." Or, if someone is a customer at a store and the cashier doesn't smile when greeting them, the customer may believe that the cashier is an "arrant buffoon" and begin to yell at them using irate and strong language.

11. Personalization

This type of distortion is especially prominent in people with clinical depression and anxiety disorders. With the personalization distortion, a person begins to take everything personally and faults themselves for everything, whether or not they had any control over the situation. There is no logic behind this distortion, and a person simply believes that everything must be their fault. For instance, a person may blame themselves because their spouse cheated on them. They may assume that even though their friends said they had a good time going out to dinner that they're lying and that the friend couldn't have had a good time because of them. Or, they may blame themselves for the foul mood of those around them, assuming it must have something to do with them.

12. Control Fallacies

With the control fallacy distortion, there are two sides to the coin, both extremes. With the first side of the coin, a person may believe that they have complete control over not only themselves but their surroundings and everything else in their lives. On the second side of the coin, a person may believe that they are only a victim in life with no control over their lives or circumstances. Both of these beliefs are incorrect and damaging extreme, which will only lead to further mistakes and distance between the person and those around them. After all, nobody has complete control of their lives just as nobody is completely powerless over their lives. We all have choices we can make, and these choices grant us a certain amount of power over our circumstances, but they don't allow us to completely control everything as if life were a series of chess moves, either. Even if life seems completely out of your control and as if there is nothing you can do, you can make choose how you approach a situation and respond.

13. Fairness Fallacy

Life simply isn't fair, which is a sad fact, but true all the same. Yes, we would all prefer to live in a life where all was fair, where good people excelled, and bad people got what was coming to them. But, life is a mixture of good and bad for all of us, and sometimes good people get the short end of the stick while bad people seem to win. With the fairness fallacy distortion a person believes everything in life should be fair, and therefore hold resentment and anger whenever they perceive unfairness. Whenever they are in a circumstance, they judge whether or not it is fair, and will then feel hopeless and anger when it falls short of being what they believe it should.

14. Change Fallacy

With the change fallacy, a person believes that others should change to their desired outcome if they are encouraged or pressured enough. This is often a direct result of a person believing that their own happiness rests in the hands of other people. They believe that they can only be happy if those around them are living in the way that they deem necessary or important. For instance, someone may believe that they can only be happy if they get their sibling to stop making certain life choices. Or, they may try to micromanage all of their coworkers thinking that if they can control the environment around them they can attain happiness.

15. Always Right

With the always right distortion, a person believes that they must always be completely right, accurate, and excel in every way. People often struggle with this distortion if they also have impostor syndrome or if they are a perfectionist. This distortion leads to people being unwilling ever to accept that they were wrong or made a mistake. They would be willing to fight for hours and never give up on the idea that they were in the wrong, made a mistake, or failed to attain perfection. For instance, someone who is always arguing with others on politics, interests, or hobbies may struggle with this distortion. These people would be willing to argue with others for hours after hours on politics or something as simple as a comic book, unable to simply "agree to disagree" because to them it is of vital importance that they are proven in the right.

16. Heaven's Reward Fallacy

You see this distortion everywhere. Its message is loudly proclaimed by people throughout our lives, on TV, and in the books, we read. It's easy to see how people might get drawn into this distortion when it feels as if it is practically everywhere they look. With the heaven's reward fallacy distortion, a person begins to believe that a person's hard work and persevering through struggles and suffering will lead to a just reward. But, the truth is, sometimes we can work hard, we can do our best, we can persevere, but we still won't attain that which we wished for. As an example, a person might try their hardest and never be able to get into their dream college or attain their dream job. Or, they may fall in love, and the other person may simply never love them back. These are all sad instances, but we need to accept that while we can work hard, it doesn't mean that we will "win" what we want. When people with this distortion are faced with this reality, they often struggle with frustration, disappointment, anger, confusion and depression.

As you can see, there are quite a number of cognitive distortions. In order to combat these distortions, it is important to learn their line of thinking and confront it. Begin to see negative thought patterns as a red flag for a potential distortion, which once you discover you can begin to unravel and turn it into a more balanced perspective. If you examine these distortions, you will find that each one deals with negativity in one way or another, which is why it is vital that you learn to examine your negativity for possible distortions rather than simply accepting it as truth.

Cognitive distortions are common, both in mentally healthy people and those with mental illnesses. No matter your individual case, if you are someone who is struggling with cognitive distortions don't underestimate the effect they may be having on your life. These inaccurate thought patterns are sneaky and can lead to great frustration, anxiety, anger, depression, and more down the road. Even if you are not struggling with these issues now, if you continue to allow cognitive distortions to fester in your life then you will find that they cause negative impacts in many areas.

Begin to notice the red flags of negativity, and before long you will be on your way to addressing the harmful cognitive distortions in your life.

Chapter 2: Turn Negativity into Positive

We all struggle with automatic thoughts. These well examined in the practice of cognitive behavioral therapy, in which it is taught that these are ideas, beliefs, or images that occur in response to a specific action, event, or another trigger. As their name implies, automatic thoughts pop into our minds without conscious effort or thought. Automatic thoughts are not either good or bad, as they can be both. For instance, you might have an automatic thought telling you to "be careful" when you are walking alone to your car at night and hear something in the distance. Or, it might tell you to stop and double check both sides of the road before crossing the street. But, these automatic thoughts when paired with cognitive distortions can lead to many negative thoughts and feelings. For instance, you may have automatic thoughts such as "I can't do this" when taking on a new challenge, or "everybody must hate me" when trying to talk to someone. These negative automatic thoughts must be challenged; otherwise, they will lead to a vicious cycle, worsen cognitive distortions, increase anxiety, and possibly even lead to depression.

With cognitive behavioral therapy, you can learn to overturn your negative automatic thoughts and distortions with healthy and balanced thinking. You can learn to analyze your thoughts, finding which are true and false, which are helpful and unhelpful, and then use that knowledge to balance out your thinking. With practice, you will learn to negate negative thoughts and replace them with healthy thoughts until it becomes second nature. As you learn to overcome your negative thought patterns, you will be able to live a happier and healthier life. You will learn to better care for yourself, those around you, and have the ability to better take on the challenges life throws at you. Over time, you will find coping with stress, anxiety, insomnia, depression, and intrusive thoughts easier and they may even greatly decrease.

Cognitive behavioral therapy will teach you the techniques and practices you need, and by using these tools consistently, you will soon find that this healthier thinking comes more naturally. For instance, instead of thinking that everyone in the room must dislike you, you can accept that there will be both people who like and dislike you and that you can choose to talk to them in the hopes of making a good impression. Another example is if you got a bad grade on a paper you could accept that you didn't do your best and tell yourself that you can work towards improving rather than degrade yourself and assume you must be a failure.

With cognitive behavioral therapy, you can learn to overturn negative and distorted thinking, teaching yourself to stay on guard against negativity. Questions such as "Can I try better in the future?", "What exactly did the person say?", "Has anyone done anything to lead me to believe they dislike me?", and "What is a more balanced perspective" can help you to adjust your thinking and turn the negative into a positive.

It's important to learn that the harsh and negative views we hold of ourselves and life aren't always the truth. Use questions and affirmations in order to help yourself notice the positive and balance out the negative, in turn overcoming your distortions. For instance, you might use affirmations to remind yourself of the positive, such as "I worked hard this past week and I did my best, and the result of my hard work is that I learned and made a good impression on those around me. I will learn from my mistakes and improve further in the future. I can enjoy my successes while also learning from my mistakes."

Cognitive behavioral uses many methods to help people overturn their negative thoughts and change the way in which they think. A few of these methods include:

- Learning to notice negative or irrational thoughts
- Stopping these thoughts in their place
- Replacing negative and irrational thoughts with positive and more balanced thoughts
- How to relax both your mind and body to decrease stress

And, this is only the tip of the iceberg. Along with these methods, you can learn to incorporate positive affirmations into your daily routine. While many people have heard of the power of positive affirmations and self-talk, they have little understanding of the science behind this method and how to harness it for their benefit. They may try saying something positive to themselves in the mirror and not notice an improvement, and therefore think it isn't for them. But, this is largely due to people being unaware of how to use positive affirmations for their benefit and an unwillingness to stick with it. If you practice using positive affirmations regularly, you will find that it can have an enormous and beneficial effect on your life and mental health. With practice, you will begin to handle stress better, view yourself in a better light, and even perceive the world as a whole differently.

In order to attain benefits from positive affirmations, it's important that you learn at a fundamental level what they are and what they are not. When you struggle with negative and damaging thoughts or beliefs and cognitive distortions you can replace them with positive affirmations. These affirmations are perceived truths which we confidently tell ourselves and remind ourselves of in order to replace the negative distortions that we are prone to struggle with.

The goal of these affirmations isn't to puff up our chests or make us believe we are superior to other people or better than we are. Instead, the goal is to foster confidence, positivity, and unwind negative lies we believe. By repeating these affirmations on a regular basis, you will be able to better accept them as truth and are then less likely to believe the negative distortions you are prone to believe. With regular practice, these affirmations can profoundly affect a person's self-confidence, optimism, positivity, and even the success they achieve. After all, a person who is confident is more likely to attain the success they seek than someone who is afraid and doesn't believe in themselves.

But, it is important to remember that affirmations on their own are not a solution to all of your problems. Instead, they are a piece of the puzzle of cognitive behavioral therapy. In order to attain the benefits of CBT, you need to employ all of the methods found within this book, and not just one or two practices.

As there are many misconceptions about positive affirmations and self-talk, let's go over a couple of these misconceptions before going into detail on how you can practice these affirmations.

The goal of these positive affirmations is not to create a blind optimism, but rather the rewrite negative thoughts, break cognitive distortions, and promote positive thinking. The affirmations needed for these benefits will vary from person to person, as many of our negative thought processes and cognitive distortions were developed during our childhood and young adult lives. While what lead to these negative ideas may be long in the past, it can still affect us greatly and need to be confronted in a constructive manner.

This is why blind optimism and phrases such as "everything is perfect," or "I won't mess up," aren't constructive or helpful. Instead, phrases such as "I am prepared, but even if I make a mistake it will be okay, and I have the tools I need to handle it," and "I choose to find joy and see the good in life." While the first options promoted a false and unattainable idea of perfection, only setting a person up for disappointment, the second acknowledges that while life may not be perfect, we can choose how we react.

Positive affirmations are also not self-deception. The purpose of these phrases isn't to make you believe that your life is free of problems, that you don't mess up, that you don't have any responsibility, or that your stress if unfounded. Instead, the purpose is to help us acknowledge that while our stress may be understandable, we also have a habit of making our stress worse than it needs to be with negative thought patterns and distortions.

With an affirmation that is true and rooted in reality, you can learn to readjust your thought process and create firm and constructive intentions. As this is the true purpose of affirmations, it explains why people who try deceiving themselves with nice-sounding thoughts never experience the benefits that positive affirmations have to offer.

While it is best to use positive affirmations in conjunction with a complete cognitive behavioral therapy approach, one of the benefits of these affirmations is that you can benefit from them beginning immediately. Even before you finish reading this book, you can begin to implement positive affirmations and self-talk in your daily life in order to change your inner dialogue from something negative to something balanced. By beginning to implement positive affirmations immediately, you can get a head start on improved emotional and mental well-being, and prepare yourself to soon begin a CBT approach to your entire life for even more benefits.

In order to start practicing positive affirmations and self-talk begin with these simple and easy-to-follow steps:

1.   Take Small Steps

When you begin the process of using positive affirmations and self-talk don't feel that you have to go from zero to one-hundred overnight. Instead, start with small steps to change your thoughts and inner dialogue. You can do this by taking note and analyzing how you react to situations and words, and then ask yourself why it elicits the emotions are you experiencing.

2.   Identify Your Negativity

When you notice that you are having negative thoughts or emotions, then take a moment to stop and acknowledge that what you are feeling is negativity and identify what emotion you are feeling. Is the emotion fear? Guilt? Doubt? Anger? Shame? By acknowledging and identifying your thoughts and feelings, you can then deal with them.

3.   Replace the Negative with Positive

After you have acknowledged and identified your negative thoughts, work towards replacing them with something more positive. For instance, rather than calling yourself an "idiot" replace it with something such as "I may have been ignorant on this matter, but I can learn and grow." If you are thinking "I'm a failure" you can replace it with "What matters is that I tried my best."

4.   Balanced and True

When using positive affirmations and self-talk, it is vital that it be balanced and true if you want it to be effective and helpful. For instance, it wouldn't be helpful to tell yourself "I will never make a mistake," as you are only setting yourself up for failure and you very well know that you will make mistakes. On the other hand, if you tell yourself "I am prepared, and I will do my best" you are reminding yourself that even if you do make a mistake, you can handle it and it will be okay. This could be compared to creating business goals, which also have to be balanced and true. You wouldn't find it helpful to say "I'm going to make a million dollars the opening week of business," but it could be helpful to say "I will network with five people every day in order to grow my business."

5.   Find Inspiration

When you are struggling with self-doubt, fear, anger, and other negative emotions it can be difficult to know what affirmations you need to help when beginning. Of course, over time it becomes easier, but at first, you are at a loss as you don't believe in yourself. But, there are many people you can reach out to for inspiration, you don't have to stand alone. Look for other people who use positive affirmations for inspiration; you don't even have to talk to them personally. You can find a wide range of positive affirmations online that you can use or adapt to your situation.

6.   Practice Regularly

If you hope to receive success and improvement from the use of positive affirmations and self-talk, you must practice on a regular day-to-day basis. After all, change doesn't happen overnight. You can't rewire your brain and thought process in a single day or even a week. Stick with using these positive affirmations, practicing using them on a daily basis for at least a month. I promise you if you follow all of these steps for a month you will notice a difference looking back. Practice using these positive affirmations when you wake up in the morning, before you go to sleep at night, and whenever you find yourself thinking negatively.

One of the wonderful aspects of positive affirmations and self-talk is that anyone can experience their benefits with a little knowledge, time, and practice. But, remember, if you hope to reap all of the benefits that positive affirmations have to offer, use them in conjunction with the other tools and practices written about in this book.

Along with using positive affirmations, you may also

try to implement cognitive restructuring, which is one of the core principles of cognitive behavioral therapy practice. Cognitive restructuring is similar to positive affirmations, and use some of the same steps, but it can be applied even more widely and have a greater benefit on cognitive distortions. To experience the most benefits, combine using both positive affirmations and cognitive restructuring.

Imagine that you write a report for school and get a pretty good grade. But, the teacher has some recommendations on how you can improve. While you may know that you did well, got a good grade, and they are only trying to help you improve, it may have hit a raw nerve. You feel upset, even though you know that you shouldn't. So, after you leave the situation you think it over, consider why you were upset and felt attacked, and then remind yourself that your teacher thought you did well and is only trying to help because they believe in you. After you take some time, you decide to take up your teacher's advice and apologize for taking out your frustrations in your conversation with them.

In this situation, you have used cognitive restructuring in order to overcome your negative thought process and emotions and change your thinking.

Cognitive restructuring is a helpful practice in order to overcome your automatic thoughts and emotions. With regular practice, you will learn how to understand your thoughts and emotions so that you can then change them into something more balanced and healthy. You can learn to overcome untrue and unhelpful negative thoughts into something that will benefit both yourself and others. This is a practice that everyone can benefit from, as even people with few cognitive distortions will at times struggle with negative and untrue automatic thoughts. Along with benefiting peoples' relationships and stress levels, cognitive restructuring has also been used in the treatment of anxiety, depression, post-traumatic stress disorder, phobias, addictions, and more.

You will find that as you use cognitive restructuring your approach to situations changes and your mood improves. This allows you to have better interactions with others and increase your productivity. When struggling with negative moods and unpleasant thoughts it's simply more difficult to interact with others and be productive, but with cognitive restructuring, you can turn this around! In order to utilize and benefit from cognitive restructuring try following these eight steps on a regular basis:

Calm Your Mind

If you are struggling with emotions, then you may have trouble confronting the thoughts behind the emotions. Therefore, first calm your mind by using deep breathing or meditation until your stress decreases and you can think more easily and calmly.

Identify the Trigger

After you have calmed down identify and describe the trigger that caused you to become upset, whether it was a specific situation or phrase.

Analyze Your Emotions

Calmly analyze your emotions and what you were feeling during the triggering circumstance. When describing your emotions and moods keep in mind that this is different from thoughts. Psychologists explain that while moods and emotions are often explainable in a single word or two, the thoughts behind these emotions are more complex and require complete sentences in order to explain. For instance, you may feel the emotions anger or humiliation, but your thoughts behind these emotions are that you are angry that your significant other made a joke at your expense in front of your friends and you now feel humiliated because of it.

Identify Your Automatic Thoughts

The automatic thoughts you are experiencing are the thoughts that you first experienced in the moment and as a reaction to your emotions. For instance, in the situation above your automatic thoughts may be:

"My significant other doesn't respect me."

"My friends think I'm weak."

"Everyone must think I'm a joke."

"I'm alone in this world."

All of these are automatic thoughts caused by the situation and emotions. But, the most disturbing or distressing thoughts are known as "hot thoughts." In this situation, the hot thoughts are *"everyone must think I'm a joke,"* and *"I'm alone in this world."*

Search for Supportive Evidence

After writing out a list of your emotions and automatic thoughts, search for objective evidence that supports these thoughts. For instance, you might write:

"My friends laughed along to the joke."

"My significant other repeatedly makes jokes at my expense."

The goal of this is to objectively look at the facts, and then write down specific circumstances that lead to your automatic thoughts.

Search for Contradictory Evidence

After searching for objective evidence that supports your automatic thoughts, it's vital that you search for objective evidence which contradicts these thoughts. In this case, this evidence might be:

"My friends seemed to have been awkwardly laughing."

"I've never seen my friends make jokes at my expense."

"My significant other is awkward when meeting people."

"I've never told my significant other that I don't like jokes at my expense."

"Both my friends and significant other are always supportive."

After looking at both lists, you can see that there is more evidence contradicting your fears and concern. It is fair to be hurt, but instead of lashing out in anger and embarrassment, it is better to calmly talk over the issue with the people involved.

Find Balanced and Fair Thoughts

By this step, you have calmed your mind and looked objectively at the situation. You should now have the ability to analyze the situation and create a more balanced and fair view about the triggering circumstance. If you are having a difficult time doing this on your own, then you may find help in discussing it with someone else and testing out your new ideas to see if they are balanced. When asking someone to listen ensure that it is someone who is also balanced and fair rather than someone who gets angry or emotional easily. Just as you did with the previous steps, be sure to write down your new views and ideas as you think of them. By writing down each step, you will have an easier time focusing and will better be able to consider new ideas. Some new and balanced ideas of the above situation might include:

"What my significant other said hurt and embarrassed me, but I know that wasn't their intent."

"I trust my friends, their laughter hurt but I'm sure that they simply did not know how to respond, I will ask them about it calmly."

"Instead of getting angry, I will calmly ask my significant other to please refrain from making jokes at my expense. Open

communication is important in every relationship."

"The joke wasn't anything negative, but it hit a raw nerve which is why it hurt. I'm sure nobody knew it caused me pain."

Analyze Your New Mood

After following the previous seven steps, you should be able to think much more clearly and have a better view of the situation. Reanalyze your mood and see if it has improved, and then write down the results of how you feel.

After you understand your new emotional state ask yourself what you can do to improve the situation. You may no longer need to take action, you may want to calmly discuss it with the other person(s) involved, or you may want to apologize if you found that you lashed out in anger.

Lastly, use positive affirmations to help yourself learn

to better react to similar situations that may occur at some point in the future.

The use of positive affirmations and cognitive restructuring is greatly beneficial in replacing negative thoughts with something more balanced and positive. It will take time, but practice using these methods on a daily basis and before long you will find that your entire thought process changes and that your cognitive distortions become more balanced.

Chapter 3: Meditate and be Mindful of Your Strengths and Weaknesses

Knowing yourself is an important part of living a healthy and full life. If you hope to overcome your weaknesses and utilize your strengths, you first must know what these include. Because of this, it's important to practice techniques in order to increase your self-awareness. Along with self-awareness, it's important to practice meditation and mindfulness, to help you see yourself honestly and without judgment. In this chapter, you will learn how to truly see yourself for who you are, without judging whether you are "good" or "bad." You will learn how to see who you truly are so that you can then come to love yourself and live your life to the fullest as the best version of yourself.

When beginning to take a deeper look at yourself, remember to do so without judgment. This can be difficult in the beginning, especially for people who struggle with depression and anxiety. But, try to remain mentally outside of yourself, looking at yourself as if you were analyzing someone else. Think about describing yourself as if you were describing a friend. In a notebook write down your strengths, weaknesses, how you act and react, your feelings, what you are passionate about, what makes you angry, and what makes you happy.

By analyzing yourself and becoming self-aware of who you truly are as an individual you will better understand your habits, desires, needs, failings, and everything else that makes you, you. This is helpful, as it will help you have a better chance of success in all that you do, interact with other people better, and learn how to better cope with life's changes and difficulties. Learning who you are without judgment allows you to empower yourself. You will have the ability to increase your strengths and overcome your weaknesses. Becoming more self-aware is the first step in improving yourself, setting goals, and making progress.

A great deal of research has been done on self-awareness, showing that it is directly linked to both a person's success and their emotional intelligence. The research has found that because you can consider your weaknesses, strengths, desires, and what drives you that you are better able to create achievable goals and attain success. Whether you are hoping to choose a field to work in that best suits your skillset or hope to anticipate possible triggers and identify ways in which to react in a more beneficial manner, self-awareness can help.

Due to the importance of self-awareness, it has a place in every form of psychotherapy, including cognitive behavioral therapy. One common exercise most used with CBT is journaling. Whenever you find yourself struggling with negative thoughts or emotions fill out your journal with answers to the following:

• Date and time of the negative experience, feelings, or thoughts.

• The situation in which the thoughts or emotions occurred.

• The automatic thoughts you experienced. These thoughts are often destructive, and therefore should be rated in how much you believe they are true. For instance, if the thought is "I'm worthless" you then need to rate it on a scale of zero to one-hundred percent in how much you agree with the thought.

• Next, write down the emotions that are tied to the automatic thought and the intensity of said emotion. For instance, the emotion with the previously mentioned thought could be despair at seventy percent intensity.

•   The fifth subject you should track is which cognitive distortion(s) is tied to your automatic thoughts and emotions. For instance, you may be struggling with personalization, polarization, or catastrophizing.

•   Finally, after you have journaled what you are struggling with, analyze the alternative and more positive thoughts that you may use to replace the negative automatic thoughts.

•   The last portion of your journaling should be your results after completing the exercise. Do you feel better? Did you resolve the situation? Do you believe in the new positive thought in place of the negative one? What are your emotions and thoughts now?

One practice regularly used in order to help people develop more self-awareness without judgment is a form of meditation known as mindfulness. This practice is regularly used in cognitive behavioral therapy to help people understand their own emotions and thoughts while staying fully present in the moment. Mindfulness can help as our thoughts influence our feelings, which then affect our behavior. Therefore, if you hope to change your behavior, you must first understand and change your thought process. This is used to treat a number of conditions, including depression, anxiety, substance abuse, and eating disorders.

By combining the practices of cognitive behavioral therapy with mindfulness (often known as MBCT when combined) a person can learn how to effectively combat and prevent negative automatic thoughts and emotions from triggering a worse and deeper state of emotional distress and harmful reactions. Using MBCT, you can learn to alter your automatic thoughts so that you do not immediately react negatively to situations and possible triggers. You will find that you can break free from your emotional and mental struggles, to help you better manage your anxiety, stress, depression, or a number of other struggles.

Mindfulness practices combined with cognitive behavioral therapy is powerful and has far-reaching beneficial effects. This is because it does not only help you to be more mindful and self-aware during your sessions of mindfulness but throughout your entire daily life. You will learn how to think outside of yourself, and better connect with the world at large. Because of this, you are much less likely to get stuck in a negative thought process or spiral down into a dark place. As you practice using mindfulness regularly, you will be better able to manage damaging depressive and anxiety-related thoughts, increasing your positive interactions and emotional state.

Some other benefits of mindfulness include:

Reduced Stress

Mindfulness is a form of meditation that utilizes self-awareness and deep breathing. Studies have shown the many great effects that deep breathing can have on the human body and mental state. One of these great benefits includes a deep calming of the mental state and nervous system, which especially helps in stressful situations.

You may also find that mindfulness decreases stress as you become more aware of the present, giving you a greater appreciation of life and helping you to evaluate your priorities. By living in the present, you naturally do not focus on your mistakes from the past or the obligations of the future, decreasing the stress related to these thoughts. Combined, these effects of mindfulness can help you both during your everyday life and during stressful situations.

Improved Mood

If you struggle with depression, you will find that mindfulness combined with cognitive behavioral therapy can have a profound effect on your daily mood. Yet, even if you don't have depression, mindfulness can increase your mood by decreasing minor feelings of sadness and reducing the effects of troublesome events.

You may find that you experience emotions of worthlessness and loss less frequently when practicing mindfulness on a daily basis, as it helps you to feel more connected to your life's purpose and those around you. With regular practice, you will be in attuned to your surroundings and learn to appreciate your everyday joys and routine better. This is because when you pay attention to a situation rather than becoming distracted by your emotions or thoughts you can better notice and understand your effect on the world around you. Lastly, practicing mindfulness on a regular basis has been shown to develop areas of the brain that increase feelings of positivity while decreasing anxiety.

Sleep Better

Many people who struggle with anxiety, stress, and depression know all too well the effects that these thoughts and emotions can have on a night's rest. But, with mindfulness meditation, **you can overcome the barriers that prevent you from sleeping** well and finally get the rest your body needs. Studies have even found that mindfulness can help those with diagnosed sleep disorders sleep better at night and reduce daytime sleepiness and impairments.

Increase Gray Matter

One of the surprising and wonderful benefits of regular mindfulness is an increase in gray matter cells in the brain. Researchers conducted brain scans before and after mindfulness practices and found that gray matter increased in the cortex, hippocampus, cerebellum, posterior cingulate cortex, and the temporoparietal junction. These regions of the brain are important for emotional regulation, learning and memory, perspective, and understanding oneself.

These benefits are only the tip of the iceberg, as there are many more scientifically-backed proven benefits of mindfulness and meditation. But, before you begin to practice mindfulness, there are some aspects of this practice that you should keep in mind.

First, it is important to know that you will be unable to silence your mind completely. But, that's okay. The goal is not to silence your mind to all around you, but instead to stay present in the moment without stress or judgment.

While you attempt to focus on your body and keeping your mind at the moment, you will most likely find that your mind wanders and numerous thoughts arise. Your mind may wander to stressors of your day, your to-do list, events that have happened, or on anything else but staying focused in the moment. You want to attempt to focus on the moment as much as possible, but it is not a failure to have a wandering mind. Having your mind wander during these moments is a completely natural and human reaction. Only people who have trained consistently for lengthy periods of time for years, such as monks, are able to prevent their minds from wandering. In fact, you will find that having your mind wander has its own benefits, as it gives you the opportunity to notice your mind has wandered and refocus yourself. During a session of mindfulness, you will find that you must bring your consciousness back to the present time and again. One of the benefits of this is that it makes it easier for you to refocus your attention at any point in the day, whether you are meditating or not. You will gradually gain better control of your focus and mental state.

An important aspect of mindfulness is looking at situations and yourself without judgment. Yet, you will likely find that assessing without judgment is much easier said than done. After all, most of us listen to our inner critics more than we should, leading us to have negative self-perceptions and anxieties. This inner critic may be helpful and needed at times, but it can also be overly critical and get in the way of development and true progress. But, if you learn to asses situations without judgment during mindfulness practice, then you will find that you are better capable of diffusing your judgment in other situations and adjusting how you react. Therefore, when you are practicing mindfulness try not to judge yourself whenever thoughts pop up and or your mind wanders. Instead, be aware that a judgment has occurred, take note or label the judgment, and then allow it to pass without holding onto it.

Whether your mind is wandering or judgments are popping into your consciousness, focus on returning your thoughts to the present time and again. Mindfulness isn't about staying present in the moment without fail, rather about constantly bringing your mind back to the present whenever it wanders. You can do this with deep breathing exercises, which help to anchor your mind and body to the present moment. You will find that over time this gets easier, as your mind will learn to recenter itself whenever you begin to use deep breathing exercises.

Steps to Practicing Mindfulness

There are multiple ways in which you can practice mindfulness. But, however you choose to attain this desired state, it is based on a deliberate and relaxed focus on sensations and thoughts while reserving judgment. By doing this while in a relaxed yet alert state, you will be able to focus on the moment in a healing manner. However, you practice mindfulness it is a form of meditation.

There are many types of meditation. The mindfulness approach focuses on concentration, on having a person focus on deep breathing exercises while allowing thoughts to come and go, always coming back to concentrate on their breathing. This can be done while standing, sitting, or laying down. But, it can also be done while practicing other exercises, such as yoga or Tai chi. These practices can increase the relaxation response, helping to reduce stress and increase concentration further. Whatever you choose to do while practicing your mindfulness, try to ensure it is a comfortable position to boost your concentration.

When beginning your mindfulness if you are struggling to calm your mind and relax, begin with an exaggerated deep breath. Inhale through your nose for three seconds, hold it for two seconds, and then exhale for four seconds. You can do this one to three times in order to relax. Afterward, observe each breath, attempting to give it your full concentration. Notice the way the air feels as it enters and exits your lungs. Pay attention to how your chest rises and falls. Focus on the way the air feels traveling through your nostrils. Your mind may wander due to thoughts that pop up or other sensations in your body, but that's okay. Whenever you notice your mind wanders simply gently bring it back to focusing on your breath.

Try to practice this for seven to ten minutes. When you are done focusing on your breathing slowly bring yourself back, focusing on your body and noticing all of its many sensations. Allow yourself to relax even more deeply and recognize the ways in which you have benefited from the mindfulness exercise.

Chapter 4: Ask for Advice: You are Not Alone

It's never easy to open up to people about our mental health. This is true both when we first open up to the people closest to us and when we choose to seek out professional mental health services. But, an important step in taking care of ourselves and our mental health lies in knowing that we are not alone and asking others for help and advice. Whether you are simply struggling with everyday stressors, an anxiety disorder, or clinical depression, opening up to your loved ones or a professional can greatly help. In fact, many people see a therapist simply to help them work through their daily stressors and to get advice, even if they don't have a mental illness. Remember, caring for your mental and emotional well-being is important for everyone and there is nothing to be ashamed of.

But, even if you consciously know that you shouldn't be ashamed, it can still be hard to open up about our inner struggles. Yet, if you choose to open up, then you can experience a wealth of benefits, including advice, reassurance, and support. This can make a great difference in a person's stress, anxiety, and depression. If you're willing to open up to your loved ones and begin a conversation about your inner struggles then you will be able to gain the help you need, realize that you aren't alone, and continue to break down walls of the stigma surrounding mental health.

First, when hoping to open up to family or friends about your inner struggles it is important to create an environment that is comfortable. Talking about these issues is hard enough; we feel vulnerable. Therefore, you want to make it as easy as possible for you to open up. This will vary from person to person, so think about what will make you most comfortable, you might try writing down a list of ideas.

You will want the location that you open up at to be accessible and comfortable. Try to find a place that won't cause you to expend extra energy to arrive at or leave, as you will already be spending a great deal of energy discussing your mental health. It is also important to consider whether there will be other people around and the noise level. For instance, a restaurant is likely not an ideal place to open up, as you will feel more self-conscious with strangers and waiters around. There will also be an increased noise level, making it possibly difficult to hear the conversation. Try to find somewhere with no other people and little noise.

Oftentimes, meeting in a home is convenient, private, and quite. Although, if you are unsure how your loved ones will respond to hearing about your mental health struggles you may want a place that is quiet yet slightly public. For instance, a quiet beach or park may be ideal in these cases.

Lastly, when choosing your location and time to

ensure that there is plenty of time available for you to talk as long as needed. You will likely want to ensure that the environment you choose is open for at least a few hours and that your loved ones have that amount of time set aside in their schedules to talk. You don't want to be in a location halfway through your discussion only for it to be closing time and you must leave. If there is a time limit, it will only pressure both you and your loved ones to rush the important conversation.

Now, it's important to know how to talk about your mental health. Remember, having mental health struggles is nothing to be self-conscious about. Everyone struggles with their mental state to some extent, whether it is from daily stressors or mental illness. And, just as you are unable to control whether you have a physical illness such as the flu or a disease, you are unable to control whether you have a mental illness. There is no reason for you to feel ashamed.

When planning to open up to your loved ones about

your inner struggles consider who your audience is. Whether you are planning to open up to family or friends, it can help first to gauge how they feel about mental illness and treatment. This can help you to prepare and know what to say and how to say it. One way you can gauge your audience is by noticing how they respond to mental illness when it is discussed on television. Knowing if they are supportive or critical can be helpful, as well as knowing if they have gone through mental illness themselves or been close to others struggling with it.

Keep these factors in consideration and think through how the conversation might go. You can plan for ideal, neutral, and negative responses, deciding how you will respond to each. By having a plan for any reaction, you will feel more confident and prepared. But, keep in mind that they might not know the same mental health-related language that you have learned, so try to prepare yourself with terms that a layman will understand.

It is definitely scary to take a risk to open up your inner struggles and thoughts; you are making yourself vulnerable. But, it's important to remember that by doing this you are giving yourself an opportunity to find support, aid, and advice from those you most care about. If you take your time and use direct language rather than vague statements you increase your chance of being heard. By speaking from your direct experiencing, using the word "I," then your loved ones should hopefully better realize your seriousness and plea for understanding. While they may not fully understand your struggles, speaking in this way they may be more empathetic and seek to further understand what you are going through.

Along with speaking with direct "I" statements, it is important to speak directly on how your mental health is affecting your life. As many people have misconceptions about mental health, it can be immensely helpful if you explain how it affects you in your daily life. By speaking in a direct manner on your personal experience rather than speaking vaguely about mental illness, your loved one may also feel less inclined to use cliched sayings or minimizing statements.

For instance, if you have depression that makes it hard to stay awake, instead of saying "my depression leaves me always tired" be more concrete. Say something such as "even if I sleep nine hours at night I still am unable to stay awake during the day. I simply am unable to move my body out of bed and have no desire to do anything." By fully explaining the problem a person is less likely to explain with a cliched "I get sleepy, too."

Before beginning your conversation, you will want to know what you are asking of the other person(s). Consider your objective and concrete ways in which you are hoping to get support or advice. After all, if you don't know how you need help, the other person can't know, either. Do you want the other person simply to offer comfort and support? Do you want them to listen without interruptions or would you prefer advice and suggestions? Do you need their help driving you to therapy or in paying for medication? Do you want them to check in on your mental health on a regular basis, to make sure you're doing okay? Have an idea of what you would like, which you can then make clear to the person or people that you are talking to. If you want them to remain quiet and listen or if you would like them to offer advice let them know this up front so that they know how to proceed throughout the conversation.

Lastly, if you are struggling to open up for your own sake, remind yourself that creating a culture in which we can easily and freely discuss mental health we are helping everyone. It's important for people to feel free to be vulnerable and authentic so that they can open up when they are struggling the most rather than relying on their own weakening resolve.

Finding Professional Help

If you decide that a mental health professional will

help you but have never gone to therapy or seen a psychiatrist previously, then you may be unsure how to go about finding help. Often times, people are at a loss when searching for a therapist, as they have no idea what standards they should meet. But, there is no reason to fear. Sometimes, it may take a few tries to find the right mental health professional to help you, but it is certainly possible. Following, we will explain how to best find the help and support you need, whether you are hoping they will help you with your daily life stress, family struggles, depression, addiction, eating disorders, or more.

There is no strict set of rules or guideline that can help you know for sure that a therapist will be the right fit. But, by having a basic understanding of the field and your requirements, you will have a better chance of finding the right therapist sooner.

First, you will want a therapist that specializes in

cognitive behavioral therapy. There are many different forms of CBT and therapists will use various tactics in helping their individual patients. But, in general, CBT is a problem-focused therapy with a short-term scheduled plan. Usually, therapists will have a set treatment schedule that lasts a period of months, and by the end of this time, their patient should greatly be benefiting from CBT.

While a therapist may discuss pains of the past with their patient, the focus should be on the present difficulties and what can help their patient in the here and now. The goal of this therapy is to teach the patient coping strategies to manage, evaluate, and deal with negative and problematic thoughts, feelings, and behaviors. Of course, a therapist may choose to combine CBT with other forms of therapy as well, such as talk therapy.

Cognitive behavioral therapy can be conducted by a

number of health professionals, the most common being psychologists, psychiatrists, and counselors. All three of these mental health professionals fall under the umbrella term "therapist." But, you may be confused as to which of these three will most help you on your journey toward healing. Don't worry! All three of these have the ability to help, but following we will explain a little more in detail about each of these so that you can better assess your needs.

• **Counselors**

A professional counselor most often has a doctoral, specialist, or master's degree from a university. A certified counselor has usually undergone and graduated training in counseling as well as passing the National Board of Certified Counselors examination. The exact licensing requirements vary based on location.

• **Psychologists**

A psychologist has graduated with a doctoral degree from a program certified by the American Psychological Association. After graduation, they must complete a one-year clinical internship as well as a two-year supervised postdoctoral position in order to attain a license.

- **Psychiatrist**

A psychiatrist has a medical degree, which allows them to practice medicine and prescribe medicines to their patients. Most often, psychiatrists will undergo a four-year medical degree, a one-year medical internship, as well as a five-year psychiatry residency program. A psychiatrist must also pass an examination from the American Board of Psychiatry and Neurology.

It's important to note that your first session with your therapist should always be a consultation. During this time you are not committing yourself to work with each other on a prolonged basis. Rather, you are coming to understand each other to find if the therapist can help you and if you feel both comfortable and confident with them. During this time, you can ask them about cognitive behavioral therapy and ensure that they are knowledgeable and well-versed in this form of therapy. You can also expect to be asked questions by your therapist, who will be trying to get to know you so that they can best understand how they can help you.

You and the therapist will most likely discuss treatment approaches, what you hope to attain from treatment, both of your goals, potential pitfalls of your goals, and possible treatment timetables.

Questions and Answers:

When you are getting to know your new therapist

there are various questions you will want them to answer. Don't hesitate to ask these questions, as it is vital that you and your therapist have a comfortable and open relationship where you are able to ask and say what you need.

While having your first consultation with a therapist, you will want to ask if they are certified or licensed by the state. If they are not, as if their care is being overseen by another certified mental health professional. While it is not necessary for using CBT, some professionals will have additional certifications in cognitive behavioral therapy, which is beneficial. You will want to ask your therapist about their focus on CBT and if they plan to use it fully in your treatment.

You may also try asking your therapist:

- How long will each session last, and how frequently will I see you?

- Which treatment methods are likely to be used?

- How long should treatment last?

- Does the therapist accept phone calls, either while at home or the office?

- If the therapist is out of town is there someone else you can contact in case of mental emergency?

- Are there any confidentiality limitations?

Remember, if a therapist doesn't answer any of your questions to your satisfaction or if you feel uncomfortable with them feel free to seek out another therapist.

As you and your therapist work together, you will decide on an individual treatment plan and approach. While your therapist can use CBT treatment methods, they may use it in conjunction with other types of therapy, as well. If there are any other forms of therapy you are interested in, such as talk therapy, you should discuss this with your therapist.

It is important to keep in mind that cognitive behavioral therapy is a skill-based therapy, in which your therapist teaches you to use various techniques out of your sessions. Therefore, in order to benefit from CBT, you must regularly practice your taught skills as your therapist instructs. If you aren't following through you can't expect benefits. You also must be honest with your therapist if you are not following through with what they tell you, as they are unable to help if you are not honest.

While you and your therapist work together, you can expect them to regularly evaluate your progress and adjust your goals to your needs. For instance, if you are not experiencing benefits or if your progress is slow your therapist may then adjust your treatment approach to better fit your needs. If this happens, it is important to ask yourself a few questions:

- Do you fully understand what your therapist is asking?

- Do the instructions given by the therapist seem relevant to your objectives?

- Do you believe that following these instructions will aid in your progression?

- Has your therapist given you alternative therapy choices?

- Has your therapist detailed any possible side effects you may experience?

Lastly, remember, if you are confused or doubt anything your therapist is telling you then question them further. Explain your confusion and ask them to better detail anything you are not understanding. A good therapist should always be willing to hear questions and to explain and discuss and confusion or dissatisfaction with you.

If you are unable to resolve your differences or confusion with your therapist, then you may want to seek out a new therapist for a second opinion. The therapist you are currently seeing should be willing to recommend someone you can consult for a second opinion. But, if they are unwilling for you to hear a second opinion, you should go ahead and move to another therapist who is more open to your needs and desires.

If you are hoping to find a therapist specifically trained and specializing in CBT, then you may try looking at the Association for Cognitive and Behavioral Therapies, Academy of Cognitive Therapy, or the American Board of Professional Psychology under the Cognitive and Behavioral Psychology section.

Whether you seek help and understanding from loved ones, mental health professionals, or both, it is an important and vital step toward gaining better mental health. These people can give you understanding, empathy, support, encouragement, advice, and walk you through your treatment.

Opening up to someone may not be easy, but in the long run, you may find that doing so has a beneficial impact on your stress, anxiety, depression, and any other mental struggles you may experience.

Chapter 5: Be Kind to Yourself

Everyone needs to be shown compassion, and that includes you. Not only is it important to treat others with compassion, but you need to use self-compassion, as well. In order to do this, you need to treat yourself with kindness, offering forgiveness and acceptance when you make mistakes or fail. When you are suffering remind yourself that it is okay, as it is a normal part of the human experience. Every person makes mistakes, we all fail, we all suffer, there is nothing to feel ashamed of, you can offer yourself forgiveness and compassion in these situations.

In these situations, you can use compassion to help make the struggles and suffering less severe. Rather than lashing out with your emotions in such situations, you can learn to comfort yourself. You can do this by offering yourself kindness rather than judgment, an acknowledgment that you are human rather than isolating yourself, and practicing mindfulness rather than over-identifying with your negative thoughts.

There are many benefits to practicing self-compassion and kindness. This practice has been shown to help people better cope with stress, increase self-awareness, and increase beneficial interpersonal relationship management. In fact, one study found that people who regularly practice self-compassion experience fewer symptoms of depression and anxiety.

One of the great things about self-compassion is that you can practice it anywhere at any time, with or without the aid of a mental health professional. If you struggle with feelings of anxiety, depression, sadness, or self-frustration, then you can begin to create habits that promote self-compassion.

You will find that there are many ways in which you can practice self-compassion. One way you can do this is that whenever you are experiencing anxiety, sadness, frustration, humiliation, or any other negative emotion directed at yourself follow this exercise. This exercise is easy to follow with only three steps, and you can use it whenever you are struggling. You will find that the more practice you have using this exercise, the more effective it is. At first, it may not seem as effective as you are unused to treating yourself with compassion. But, as you learn to be more kind to yourself, you will better be able to make use of this exercise fully.

- **Step One:**

    Acknowledge the discomfort or pain you are experiencing. You can do this in a variety of ways, such as saying "I am in pain," "I am struggling," or "I am suffering at this moment."

- **Step Two:**

Acknowledge that you are human. You can do this step by saying "everyone experiences hardships" or "struggle is a normal part of life."

- **Step Three:**

- Place your hand over your heart and express self-compassion by saying "I may be kind to myself."

One important approach in cognitive behavioral therapy for practicing self-compassion and kindness is focused on increasing curiosity while decreasing judgment. As fear and judgment have a tendency to hold people back from living to their fullest potential, replacing them with curiosity and compassion can turn your life around for the better.

When people live in a state of fear and judgment they often avoid forming deep relationships with others, following their dreams, and develop a deep inner turmoil. While we hope that by wrapping ourselves up in a cloak of fear and judgment we will protect ourselves, the truth is, in fact, the opposite. This cloak only causes us harm, and we can only achieve our hearts' desires by releasing this cloak and coming into the light of compassion.

Thankfully, no matter how ingrained you are into a habit of fear and judgment, you can release the cloak and come into the light. This is one way in which cognitive behavioral therapy excels, as it teaches you to understand yourself and your surroundings without judgment. Using the tools of CBT, such as meditation, journaling, and deep breathing, you can overcome your inner struggles. Everyone's journey will be different, and some will take longer than others, but you can overcome your ingrained struggles.

Irritability anxiety, moodiness, low self-esteem, depression, anger, and many other strong emotions are often the result of an overly critical mind rooted in fear and judgment. Although, there are many other emotional manifestations, as well. Sadly, many people are taught growing up to be self-critical and negative, making it second nature. They relate to the world through the very thought processes that are doing them harm. Thankfully, this can be unraveled with time and the right tools. It will take consistent practice, but if you are persistent, then you will experience the fruits of your labor.

While "fear" is straight forward and easy to understand, you might be confused about the term "judgment." It's important to know that all types of judgment are not negative. When a judgment is referring to being discerning, perceptive, insightful, knowledgeable, prudence, and wisdom, then it is most certainly a well-sought attribute to use throughout your life. But, when discussing fear and judgment, we are referring to something more harmful. This type of judgment involves apprehension, suspicion, anxiety, and tension. With this negative form of judgment people frequently view themselves and the world around them in a poor light. They view life as being either good or bad. They may even view life as being either bad or worse. When a person struggles with this sense of judgment, they frequently distrust or dislike themselves, which then colors their view of the people and world around them.

If you learn to replace judgment with curiosity you can create a more balanced perspective lit by a sense of clarity. While judgment leads a person to see the negative and miss pieces of the important puzzle, with curiosity you are more likely to discover all the pieces and see them in their true light rather than in a negative light. This sense of curiosity will help you find your own self-compassion and inner kindness, allowing you to shine.

In order to decrease your judgment and increase your curiosity, you can try this simple exercise, known as the Curiosity/Judgment exercise. Whenever you use the Curiosity/Judgment exercise, you begin by identifying any judgmental thoughts you may have. After identifying these thoughts, find curiosity-based thoughts in response. While it may be in your nature to judge yourself for perceived failure, be sure not to judge yourself for having judgmental thoughts. Remember, you are still working to overcome this thought process, and it will take time. That's okay. Allow yourself to release the thoughts and calmly replace them without fear or judgment.

Let's look at some examples of the Curiosity/Judgment exercise:

Example One

Judgment: *I'm a terrible artist.*

Curiosity: *Why do I think I'm a terrible artist? Where does this thought originate from? Should I try a different form of art? Do I simply need more practice? Do I enjoy making art, despite the end results? Is it good enough to simply enjoy creating art?*

Example Two

Judgment: *I'm not smart enough to go to college.*

Curiosity: *Why not try to get into college? I can see what happens once I'm actually there. What will happen if I study hard? When do I find myself most confident in my capabilities? Maybe I can talk to a friend about their college experience for advice? How do I know I'm unable to do it until I try?*

Example Three

Judgment: *That waitress must be lazy and not care about her job.*

Curiosity: *I wonder why else they could be acting that way? Could they be having a bad day? Could they be feeling poorly? Could they have been treated unkindly or have gotten bad news? What circumstances might cause a person to act this way?*

Results

After you complete this exercise, preferably by writing it down on paper, notice how you are thinking and feeling. While you may choose to do this solely in your mind, but completing in on paper you will find that you experience greater clarity and perspective. If you are unsure if a thought is based in judgment or not, try looking over the list of cognitive distortions and consider whether or not the thought might be based in a distortion.

Lastly, remember that there are two forms of judgment. The type based on reflection, wisdom, and consideration is helpful and good. The only problem is judgmental thinking that leads to tension, negative thoughts, and preconceived notions.

Additional Methods to Release Judgment and Increase Self-Compassion

If you find yourself struggling with thoughts of fear and judgment it is important to break the cycle and learn to replace them with curiosity, self-compassion, and kindness. In order to break this cycle, you must decide to change, and put in the consistent effort to use tools that will benefit your long-term health. The methods you can use to fight off the judgment and fear are simple to use, but they will only be effective if you use them consistently and regularly. It is not always easy to face your fear and judgment. But, if you choose to face it now you will experience many benefits.

1. Mindfulness:

Practicing mindfulness regularly and becoming aware and mindful of your thoughts is a vital step in becoming aware of and releasing the judgment and fear you might be holding onto. This is because as you become more aware of your body, emotions, thoughts, and the world around you, it becomes easier to release fear. When judgmental thoughts occur, you can practice mindfulness exercises to realize that they are simply thoughts created by your mind, and might not be true facts. It can help to directly label such thoughts, reminding yourself that they are in fact "judgments." This will allow you to experience thoughts and emotions without the need to act on them impulsively. Observe your negative, fearful, and judgmental thoughts and then release them.

2. Reframe Judgments and Consider the Consequences:

When you are practicing mindful awareness of your thoughts and the present, allow yourself to step back when you notice judgments occur. By stepping back, you will allow yourself to examine these thoughts and their true meaning. Without thinking negatively or catastrophizing consider what the potential consequences may occur as a result of the actions being taken.

Fears often occur due to catastrophizing and worrying about what might happen if you do or don't follow through with a certain action. Therefore, if you calmly and without fear or judgment consider realistic consequences you might be able to overturn your fear and prevent yourself from reacting in a knee-jerk manner.

3. Reframe Judgments and Increase Appreciation and Understanding: Another helpful way to reframe judgmental thoughts is to turn them around and consider how you might positively grow or find a deeper appreciation as a result of these thoughts. For instance, if you find yourself judgmentally thinking "their art is so much better than mine. I'm a failure," you can reframe this thought. Don't allow this thought to remain in such a negative light that causes you and others suffering.

Instead, take a step back, and you can reframe this judgment as "they seem like a really practiced and knowledgeable artist. I admire them and can learn how to develop my own art further."

4. Increase Validation:

Negative judgmental thoughts often occur as a way to either invalidate ourselves or others in one way or another. For instance, these thoughts often occur as "I have this negative quality due to [perceived weakness.]"

If you find yourself thinking in this way, either about yourself or others, then try to find ways in which you can release the judgment and transform it into validation. An example of this is that if you find yourself thinking "I'm a failure" you can transform it into a more validating *"Change and progress take time. I will continue to work towards my goal while being patient and compassionate towards myself."*

By reframing these thoughts into something

validating you are treating yourself with compassion and kindness. With practice, you will find that you create a new relationship with your mind and are able to treat yourself with kindness more consistently.

Part Two:

How to Overcoming Negative Thinking

Chapter 6: Recognize and Step Back from Negative Thought Patterns

There has been much study on cognitive distortions, the inaccurate and harmful thinking patterns that lead to negativity and unhappiness. While we categorize sixteen types of distorted thinking, as written about by one of the leaders in cognitive behavioral therapy, some people have estimated that there can be up to fifty types of cognitive distortions. Yet, it can be quite difficult to make a complete list of these distortions, as many of them overlap with each other. For instance, both catastrophizing and jumping to conclusions involves a person magnifying a problem unnecessarily.

Let's look at an example to understand how these cognitive distortions can overlap fully. Imagine an anxious and shy adult who is generally uncomfortable around people. They are beginning a new job, but this job entails interacting with not only new coworkers but customers, as well. This person may think:

"If I interact with people they may think I'm incompetent and laugh behind my back. I will be too humiliated to continue working, and then I'll be fired and won't be able to pay my bills."

This person is thinking on an emotional level. They are anxious about their social interactions and competence level, which leads them to emotionally reason that people will laugh behind their back. They then begin to jump to conclusions, magnify, and catastrophize the situation, believing that they will be humiliated and unable to show their face. This fear then leads to them believing that they will be out of a job and unable to keep up with their bill payments.

These fears also illustrate black and white thinking, where the person believes the experience will be all bad with no room for good outcomes. They are also struggling with the fortune telling distortion by trying to assume what will happen with little evidence. But, the primary distortion they are struggling with is emotional reasoning, as many of the unsupported and inaccurate negative thoughts arise from feelings of extreme anxiety.

With all of these cognitive distortions arising from negative emotions and thoughts, what can be done to help sort through it and take a step back? There's no one simple way out of this negativity; after all, it is easy to fall into self-sabotaging thought patterns. But, if you use cognitive behavioral therapy tools and approaches consistently on a regular basis then you will find that before long your thought patterns change and it becomes easier. It isn't easy to challenge your own thought processes and habits. Yet, if you practice doing this time and again then you will achieve the success you desire. You will find yourself with a new healthier thought process that isn't based in negativity, fear, and anxieties.

This progress can be achieved as cognitive behavioral therapy is based in providing people with a way to gain internal distance from their negative thoughts and emotions so that they can better analyze them, understand which thoughts are distorted, and then challenge these distortions. With CBT you can learn to replace a negative, emotion-fueled, and impulsive thought with one that is more rational, balanced, and true. After developing a habit of testing which thoughts are true and which are false you will more easily understand the validity of your thoughts without much conscious effort.

Imagine again our anxious person who is starting a new job. If they are able to learn tools to take a step back from their negative thought patterns and anxieties, then they may be able to challenge their irrational beliefs. By confronting their anxiety and negative thoughts with clear, balanced, and truthful statements and questions that have supporting evidence they can overturn the negativity and see that there is nothing but lies behind the fear. Once the negativity is revealed to have no basis, then it has no hold on the person and they can feel confident in the truth that they have discovered.

Are they really incompetent? Why would people think that they are incompetent? Even if they make a mistake, would everyone really laugh at them? Are these expectations accurate? No, they aren't. Upon realizing this, the person may think:

"At my previous jobs, even if I made a mistake people didn't laugh at me. People haven't acted as if I'm incompetent. In fact, I can usually do my work without attracting any negative attention."

As the person begins to unravel the lies and see the truth they will be able to continue making more true statements which support that they have nothing to be afraid of. These statements prove that the negative thoughts and anxieties have no base in reality, and therefore there is no reason to be afraid.

Along with challenging the likelihood of being incompetent and laughed at, the person may also choose to test the validity of their fears. They might accept that even if they aren't laughed at out loud, that they may still feel embarrassed and self-conscious while at work. In this case, they can challenge the embarrassment expectations. How can they do this? By telling themselves that it doesn't matter. Of course, simply saying "it doesn't matter," won't help anyone feel better. This is why they must follow it up with an accurate and true assessment of if the job will actually lead to them feeling constant self-conscious and embarrassed. They might remind themselves that their jobs have made them feel self-conscious at times in the past, but it wasn't all bad. These feelings didn't prevent them from making friends with coworkers and competently handling their job. The person might remind themselves they've been embarrassed at work before, but it didn't stop them from going to their job on a daily basis, and it didn't lead to them feeling embarrassed on a daily basis. They were still able to find ways to enjoy parts of their job and do what was expected of them. With rational and balanced statements such as these, the person may be able to challenge the idea that any embarrassment will be nearly as bad as their perceive. They can realize that even if they do become embarrassed, it won't lead to any long-lasting consequences. By reminding themselves that it doesn't matter if something embarrassing happens, they can realize that while sometimes difficult situations do occur, the resulting outcome is rarely as catastrophic as we imagine.

We all struggle with cognitive distortions, sometimes on a daily basis. Just as the human brain can think with clear fact-based logic, it can also think in an emotionally-driven cycle with little to no evidence to back up its fears. But, by finding the strength to challenge your own negative thoughts, you can overturn harmful thought patterns and replace them with healthy thinking.

By learning to adopt healthier thinking patterns you can learn to which thoughts of yours are helpful and which are unhelpful. This, in turn, can help you know how they affect your feelings and how you respond to problems that might be troubling you. With regular practice, you can learn to adopt helpful and true thoughts in place of negative and anxiety-inducing thoughts which only serve to discourage you. As you are better able to stop negative thoughts, you will find that you are better at caring for yourself, helping others, and taking life's challenges as they come at you. Better yet, you will find that your mental health improves, helping you to reduce anxiety, manage depression, cope with stress, improve sleep, and better manage your body weight. Healthy thinking and taking a step back to examine your negative emotions require you first to calm your mind and body. Cognitive behavioral therapy greatly focuses on techniques which can aid in this, such as yoga, meditation, mindfulness, journaling, muscle relaxation, and more. In order to fully practice CBT, you should use these methods and techniques on a daily basis, as this is how you will get to a place where healthy thinking becomes a natural thought process. Instead of focusing on the negative, you will find it natural to consider positive and neutral alternatives. With regular practice, negative thoughts and anxieties will no longer control your life or your mind.

Guesses Rather than Fact

Many people begin using cognitive behavioral therapy specifically to help them better manage and control their thoughts and emotions. Although, there are also many people who use this therapy to help control their addictions and other destructive behaviors and patterns. One of the most powerful ways to help people to learn to step back and control these thoughts is to treat their automatic thoughts as guesses rather than fact.

Living in the world, we all naturally have thoughts about our surroundings, ourselves, our various relationships, the past we have lived through, and the future we are preparing for. Having the ability to think such thoughts give us an understanding of the world around us and help us know how to respond to situations. It is this ability that allows us to create, solve problems, manage our day to day living, and improve our lives. But, just as these thoughts can be a powerful tool in helping us to excel, they can also be our downfall. If we live in negative thought patterns we can end up suffering, self-sabotaging, and creating more problems for ourselves.

This is especially common in people suffering from the emotional and mental strain from anxiety disorders, clinical depression, bipolar disorder, and other mental illnesses. Remember, there is nothing to be ashamed of if you have a mental illness, just as the flu or a broken leg is nothing to be ashamed of. But, sadly for people living with these conditions, they tend to get stuck in negative thought cycles which are pessimistic and get in the way of their daily lives.

Frequently, people with anxiety disorders will catastrophize their situations, overestimating the danger or negative impact situations have had or might possibly have in the future. As people with mental illnesses continue to have these thoughts they get sucked deeper and deeper into a cycle of pain and negativity, which becomes increasingly difficult to get out of. But, with CBT methods these people can slowly replace their negative thought processes with positive, pulling themselves out of the hole of pain and negativity. As time goes on and they continue to practice their new positive thought process will become second nature.

A common technique for negative thinking, especially in relation to "fortune telling," "jumping to conclusions," and "catastrophizing," is to treat your thoughts not as fact, but as guesses. This works because, the truth is, many of our thoughts are based on our feelings and pasts. This makes the thoughts simply conclusions we have come to, not accurate facts. As an example, if you are struggling with a specific new class in college, you may assume that it is too difficult and you simply are unable to succeed. This can lead to thought processes such as "I can't do this," leading you to give up.

But, if you take the thought that you are unable to succeed as a guess rather than a fact, then you are more likely to stick with the class and form an opinion after you have given it your all. Over time, you may find that you are much better at the class than you first expected. By treating this as a guess you don't become discouraged or overwhelmed, rather it is an opportunity to test out what you are good at.

Confusing thoughts and guesses with facts can be extremely damaging to your thought processes, self-esteem, and success. Keep in mind to always check your thoughts and don't automatically believe them to be true facts.

To begin thinking of your thoughts as guesses rather than fact try using alternative explanations. For instance, in the example above of someone who is struggling with a new college class, they may adjust their thinking to:

- *"This is only the beginning of the class, with time and repetition it will likely get easier."*

- *"The class may be difficult because it is new and unfamiliar, making it appear more difficult than it actually is."*

- *"While the class may be difficult, that doesn't mean I am unable to learn. I will simply have to work harder than I first believed."*

- *"New subjects are often more difficult in the beginning. If I give it time, I can later on assess my ability after I have a better understanding of the subject."*

- *"Even if it is difficult and I can't do the class perfectly, it is worth the effort. There are reasons I need to learn this material, regardless of whether or not it is easy."*

You will find that by learning to treat your automatic thoughts as only one possible guess rather than a fact it will help prevent you from rigidly holding onto a negative idea. This will help you to think more flexibly so that you can come up with more balanced and healthy perspectives. When you think flexibly with the ability to consider multiple possibilities you will find it easier to choose to consider the most effective idea. In this case, the more effective idea is that you should stick with the class and try it out rather than giving it up.

When you find yourself especially struggling, despite trying the above method, try one or more of the following techniques:

1. When you find yourself feeling strong negative emotions such as anxiety, anger, or sadness take a moment and stop. Identify the thoughts you are struggling with which seem to be most responsible for the strong emotions you are feeling.

2. Find the thought which seems to affect you the most. Remember, this thought s only one way of thinking about the available information, and it is not necessarily a fact.

3. Consider and many other possible hypotheses as you can, even if you don't believe them or think of them as fact. This will help you think more flexibly. Write these hypotheses down.

4. Choose a few hypotheses that appear the most helpful. Write down how you might act or feel differently if you adopt the hypotheses as fact.

5. After you analyze the most helpful hypotheses decide on which one is the most helpful once applied to your situation. After you have decided, continue to remind yourself of this thought as frequently you can on repeat. By doing this you can't expect the negative

thoughts to disappear, but they will reduce and become less dominant. Over time, you will find that the new healthier thought takes hold and becomes easier to believe, positively affecting your feelings and behavior.

You may also find help in realizing that the negative thoughts are simply boring. This may not help everyone. But, consider your negative thoughts as an annoying acquaintance who is always coming to you to complain. You wouldn't put up with this person on a daily basis. You would get bored and tune them out or tell them to complain to someone else. The thing is, you can do the same with your negative thoughts.

Whenever you find yourself having repeated negative automatic thoughts simply tell yourself that it's annoying. You can roll your eyes, and say "oh, it's simply the same boring thoughts again." By doing this, you recognize that not all of these thoughts are important and that it's okay to let them go.

If you struggle with thoughts about what you should and shouldn't do, then you can learn to change your approach to these thoughts. This can be especially helpful if you are someone who struggles with addiction or procrastination.

For instance, the phrase "I should exercise," implies that you don't really want to follow through, that you are making yourself exercise. This may be true, but in order to change your behaviors you need first to change your thought process. Therefore, change what you tell yourself with something such as:

- *It is important for me to stay healthy and exercise.*
- *It is best for me if I exercise*
- *I look forward to completing my exercise*
- *I like the way I feel after accomplishing my exercise.*

While these expressions might feel hollow at first, you will find that with time they begin to ring true and your exercise becomes a new habit. It becomes not about what you should or shouldn't do, but about doing what is best for you in the long-run.

You can use this when you shouldn't do something, as well. For instance, instead of saying "I shouldn't drink," you can say:

- *I choose not to drink.*
- *I am proud of myself for not drinking.*
- *I like the way I feel when I don't drink.*
- *Drinking is not a part of my life.*

Using these methods and thought patterns you can take a step back and improve your thinking. By changing your thought patterns, you can then change your feelings and your actions. Before long, you will find it is much easier to step back from your negative thoughts and adopt new more positive and helpful thoughts in their place.

Chapter 7: Coming to Your Senses

If you hope to come to your senses with cognitive behavioral therapy, it helps to have a scientific understanding of how this therapy can benefit you. By seeing the facts, you will better be able to believe in the results, which will then help you to consistently stick to using the CBT practices on a daily basis. There are many amazing benefits of CBT which can help you come to your senses and better live your life. It can do this as it not only affects the way you think and your mood, but this therapy changes your brain and the way in which it operates at a cellular level. The truth is that many studies have been done on this, proving its effectiveness.

One such study, conducted in Sweden at Linköping University, was conducted on a group of participants who were all receiving CBT online with a therapist.

The researchers focused on social anxiety disorder for this study. This form of anxiety is one of the most prominent mental illnesses, with approximately fifteen million Americans living with the condition. The researchers conducted magnetic resonance imaging (MRI) tests on the participants both prior to beginning their therapeutic treatments and after the completion of the full CBT treatment schedule. The first set of MRI scans found that people who have social anxiety disorder also have a change in the volume of their brains, as well as increased activity in the amygdala. This is important, as the amygdala is the portion of the brain which humans primarily use in emotional responses, processing memories, and making decisions. It is obvious as to why increased activity in this area of the brain would cause problems for people.

Thankfully, despite this problem affecting our biological and cellular state, there are ways in which CBT can help. Amazingly, the second set of MRI imaging found that after nine weeks of therapy the scans had improved. The participants experienced both a decrease in their brain volume and a reduction in their amygdala activity, returning it closer to normal levels. These scans also revealed that the patients who experienced the most improvement in anxiety also improved the most on the scans. This study proves that cognitive behavioral therapy is more than positive thinking; it, in fact, has the power to change your brain matter and activity. The change can affect your mood, decision making, reactions, thoughts, feelings, how you perceive the world, how your brain reacts to stimuli, and even the volume of your brain.

Cognitive behavioral therapy does not only show beneficial effects on anxiety but other mental illnesses, as well. In fact, people diagnosed with clinical depression found twice the help with CBT than they did when using antidepressants. This greatly helped prevent depressive relapse in participants. Light was shed on this shocking improvement when researchers conducted brain scans on the participants.

It turns out that CBT and antidepressants both target different areas of the brain when treating depression. While antidepressants reduce activity in the emotional center of the brain (the limbic system), CBT was found to calm the area of the brain required for reasoning (the cortex).

The results of this study found that while antidepressants may help to reduce emotions, CBT helps in a more proactive manner. This is because this form of therapy enables the brain to better process information and make decisions in a more healthy manner.

While CBT certainly involves replacing negative thoughts with positive, it is not a simple matter of "thinking positively." If you have shared your struggle with doubts and anxieties openly, then you have most likely heard the exasperating phrase *"just think positively."* This may turn some people away from CBT, but let me assure you, cognitive behavioral therapy is about much more than positive thinking. This form of therapy requires many thought, feeling, and lifestyle changes which work together to change the brain at the cellular level. This change, in turn, improves your thoughts and feelings at a base level. Don't worry, if you are depressed, anxious, or suffering from the effects of long passed trauma you are not alone. CBT has traditionally been used to help people just like you improve their lives and find contentment. This therapy does not recommend phrases as *"just think positively,"* as if you try to use such a simple approach you won't find any long-lasting benefits.

Instead of simply thinking positively, it is important to focus on using your mind in the same way as you would a tool. As you learn to use your mind in this way you can better analyze information flexibly from various angles while controlling your emotions. When you use your mind in this way to calmly and flexibly consider situations from all sides, then you can gain a sense of understanding, find solutions, and lower stress.

Imagine using your mind in this way. If you are someone with anxiety about driving, then simply telling yourself "I'm fine, I don't have anxiety," wouldn't benefit you in any way. This statement is unrealistic, untrue, and only going to fail you when it counts. As you drive and begin to feel more anxiety, you will only believe that you have somehow failed. Once you begin to feel more negatively, it is a downward spiral, and you will only continue to become more stressed until you believe that positive thinking is useless.

Therefore, rather than giving yourself a quick clique you can step back and calmly see the situation from all sides as you come to your senses. Doing this allows you to be present, rather than in a state of worry about what might happen. While you are analyzing the situation, find a solution as to what you will do if you begin to feel anxious while driving. If possible, think of multiple options to counteract various sources of anxiety. After you have a solid plan, you can then affirm yourself with positive affirmations and deep breathing exercises to calm your mind. You will be able to trust in yourself and your plan to get you through the situation because you know that even if you become anxious you have a plan that will help.

You can come to your senses out of a negative cycle by calming your mind and body through meditation or mindfulness, analyzing the situation, testing out your thoughts, considering alternatives, and then prioritizing making truthful choices rather than emotional reactions. This will naturally lead to improved mental health, especially when combined with other CBT methods and components. Keep in mind that CBT is not one single component, but rather many components working together as though they were pieces in a clock.

One powerful way to come to your senses is to conduct behavioral experiments. This practice is regularly recommended by CBT specialized therapists. Behavioral experiments are used in order to test out your negative automatic thoughts. After testing the thoughts, you can then re-evaluate the beliefs behind them and your assumptions. Over time, you will find that as you test these thoughts you can become more aware of your surroundings and have a better more solid perception of the world around you.

Behavioral experiments can help in other ways, as well. For instance, they can decrease wallowing in negative thoughts, encourage consciously processing your thoughts and assumptions, increase the memory of positive experiments, and move the mind away from negative ideas. This entire process helps a person better see the objective truth rather than their preconceived assumptions, fears, and ideas. You may be wondering how you can participate in using these powerful behavioral experiments. One of the great things about these experiments is that while they can have a profound effect, they are a simple process that you can do anywhere and at any time. Let's look at a couple of behavioral experiments to have an idea of what they can look like for different people in various situations.

Example One

Problem:A person believes that nothing can help their depression, so why even try treatment options? They don't want to even hear about medical or psychological treatment options.

Target Cognition: Therapy and medication won't help.

Alternative Perspective: Treatment may be worth trying.

Experiment: The person tries a consultation with a

cognitive behavioral therapy specialist. They discuss a multi-month treatment plan option, possible concerns, optimal outcomes, medication options, and symptoms. The therapist encourages the person to experiment with a couple of exercises to lessen their depression. First, the therapist asks the person to rate how depressed they were feeling at the moment on a scale of zero to one-hundred, with the higher the number meaning the worse the depression. The person rated their depression and then followed the therapist's instructions on deep breathing and mindfulness exercises. The therapist then walked the person through analyzing their thoughts about the stressful situation and replacing negative thoughts with more balanced perspectives. Afterward, the person was asked to rate their mood again.

Results: The person found that while they were thinking about their problems in their usual manner that their depression worsened. But, when they followed the therapist's advice and practiced the tools given to them the depression lessened, their mood lifted, and it was easier to make decisions.

Reflection: After the behavioral experiment, the person was able to see that they were living in a terrible cycle of negative thoughts and perceptions, which was coloring their view of the world and themselves. When they lived, as usual, their depression worsened, and they wished to hide in bed. But, when they followed the therapist's suggestions they felt better and hopeful. Therefore, while still a little doubtful of the benefits of therapy, the person decided to stick with it and continue following the therapist's instructions. They decided to approach treatment with an open mind, willing to follow through until the end of the treatment plan. During this time, they carefully tracked their progress in a journal and were able to see the improvement they were making every week easily.

Tip: Using behavioral experiments that center on distraction with meditation or mindfulness a person can better understand their own mood. This can also help to stop negative thoughts and refocus the mind on positive thoughts. However, it is important to remember that this will not solve or remove the underlying depression. This is simply one tool to use in the complete CBT model.

Example Two

Problem: This person struggles with severe obsessive-compulsive disorder (OCD) and feels that if they don't follow through with their compulsions that something bad will happen. They cannot say exactly what will happen, but it is completely terrifying and overwhelming.

Target Cognition: If they don't test the stove knobs fifteen times before leaving the house or going to sleep the entire house will burn down.

Alternative Perspective: They can check the stove once to see if it is off before going to sleep or leaving the house.

Experiment: To help decrease the anxiety from the OCD the experiment is carried out in steps. During the first step, the person was instructed to check the stove knob once before going to the opposite side of the house and remaining there for a lengthy period of time.

During the second phase of the experiment, the person checked the stove knob once, took a picture on their phone proving that it was off, and then went to sleep for the night. They repeated these steps again but left the house the following time. If they became anxious that maybe the stove was somehow on, they would look at the picture and remind themselves that they had, in fact, turned it off.

After getting used to the second phase of the experiment the person left the house with only checking the stove knob once and not taking a picture of it. They left the house for only fifteen minutes but gradually worked up to longer outings until they could be out all day.

Results: After slowly walking through the experiment in steps, the person was able to leave the house with only checking the stove's knob once rather than fifteen times. During this time, as they took the test slowly, they were able to complete the experiment with minimal anxiety.

Reflection: After completing the experiment the person was able to gain confidence in themselves and in CBT. While the experiments take time and energy, they had the courage to continue practicing behavioral experiments to overcome various anxieties and compulsions. They felt more at ease and less anxious, as they were able to decrease the number of compulsions they were struggling with.

Centering Yourself and Silencing the Inner Critic

Lastly, a vital piece in the puzzle when coming to your senses is silencing your inner critic. This critic is more severe than any critic on the outside may be, and we often allow it to control our lives. By listening to this critic, we are allowing it to smother our potential and decrease our belief in ourselves. But, if you learn how to silence this critic you will find that you can see yourself and the world around you in a new light. You will be able to see more clearly as if waking up from the night for the first time and seeing the light of the dawn.

In order to silence your inner critic, try following these four steps:

Notice Your Critic

If you hope to gain control of your inner critic, you can only do so if you first notice it. We are always having a conversation within ourselves. This happens whether we are asleep or awake, but we can most control and be aware of this critic while we are awake. Many people are unaware of this critic, as the conversations we have with ourselves are rapid and automatic. These happen so quickly that you hardly have the time to notice one thought before your brain moves onto the next. Therefore, in order to notice your inner critic, you must make a conscious and steady effort to be aware of your thoughts. Slow your pace down and focus on paying more attention to your various thoughts and emotions throughout your day. You will find that whenever you feel negative emotions your inner critic will be working overtime. These are the times when you should pay especially close attention to how your inner critic is affecting you. When you notice self-critical thoughts try to write them down in either a notebook or on your phone. Do this for a week, so that you or your therapist can have a better idea of what you are dealing with. Every time you notice yourself being self-critical write down one or two words about the situation.

For instance, you may write "I'm lazy; I don't want to get out of bed; there is no point in doing anything." Once you become aware of what your inner voice is saying, you will be ready to combat the thoughts.

Separate the Critic from Yourself

Your inner critic can thrive when you don't notice it. For this reason, it wants to remain hidden, slowly causing you harm. Yet, you were not born with this critic. Babies are free from this critic, and only develop it after they have internalized outside voices. For instance, they might internalize expectations placed on them, standards, and the criticisms they hear from others. Therefore, work on separating your inner critic from yourself. You are not the critic, and the critic is not you. To help in doing this, give the inner critic a name, such as Jerk Face or The Annoying Nag. It doesn't matter what the name is, just that you use it to separate the critic from yourself. By doing this, you are freeing yourself from its influence and criticism.

Confront the Critic

You can't simply ignore your inner critic; you must confront it in order to take away the power it holds over you. How can you do this? Simply by telling your inner critic, whatever you have named it, that you don't wish to hear from it can have a surprising amount of power. Whenever you hear this inner critic begin to nag at you, try telling it to be silent or go away. Refuse to listen to a single word uttered. You can tell your inner critic that you know it's a liar and that rather than listening to it you choose to demonstrate self-kindness and compassion.

Replace the Inner Critic

Rather than simply ignoring your inner critic, you

can best fight it off if you completely replace it. This way, rather than struggling with self-critical thoughts, you can create a strong and powerful ally that focuses on self-compassion. Imagine this new voice as being a close friend who supports and cares for you. But, in order to create this new compassionate inner voice, you must learn how to recognize your positive traits. Don't be discouraged if it takes time to notice your positive traits. Our brains work with selective filtering, which always looks for evidence to support what we believe about ourselves to be true. For instance, if you believe that you are a failure, you will constantly look for small ways in which you have "failed," even if you usually are quite a successful person. Any small mistake you make will be deemed as proof that you are a failure. You can create your new self-compassionate voice by deliberately telling yourself kind truths. For instance, if you hear the inner critic telling yourself that you are a failure again, you first confront the critic, telling it to be quiet. Then, you replace the negative thoughts with something more compassionate, such as "I have capable." After making this statement search and find as many instances that support the new kinder statement as possible. The more examples you are able to find that prove that you are capable, the less power the inner critic will have over you. As you continue to practice this consistently, the inner critic will come around less frequently.

Chapter 8: Regular Mindfulness Practice

Most of us live quite busy lives. Between jobs, school, housecleaning, shopping, social events, family obligations, and required time to eat and sleep we are nearly constantly doing something. During this daily rush that lasts one week after the next, we lose connection with ourselves and the present moment. You begin to lose track of your own mental state and how you are doing. For instance, you will rarely notice how you are feeling as you complete tasks, as you are focused on what you are doing and what you have to do next.

Thankfully, there are ways in which you can re-center yourself during the business and find yourself in the present moment. You can understand and accept yourself without judgment. This practice is incredibly impressive, with a large number of scientific studies finding that it can reduce stress and increase a person's overall life happiness.

Some other benefits of regularly practicing mindfulness include:

- **Increased Mental Health**
  Mindfulness is regularly used during the process of therapy in order to treat a number of conditions, struggles, and conflicts. Some of the situations that mindfulness can improve mental health include when used with depression, anxiety disorders, substance abuse, obsessive-compulsive disorder, couples therapy, eating disorders, bipolar disorder, and more.

- **Increased Physical Health**
  Surprisingly to many people, but well understood by therapists, is the power of mindfulness can increase a person's physical health, along with their mental health. For instance, regular use of this practice may improve sleep, lower blood pressure, treat

heart disease, improve gastrointestinal symptoms, and lower chronic pain.

- **Increase Overall Well-Being**
  By using mindfulness regularly, you will learn how to increase self-compassion, release judgment, calm the mind, and release stress. By regularly using this practice in your daily life you will find that you are more satisfied and can more fully and easily enjoy the pleasures of life as they occur. You will have the ability to more fully engage with others and in activities while also being more capable when dealing with difficult events. As mindfulness teaches people to focus on the present, it becomes easier to avoid getting caught on in stress, worries, and regrets. This then helps to increase your self-esteem and kindness, allowing you to know yourself better and connect more deeply with others.

There are many different mindfulness practices you can use. Please, try multiple varieties and find what works best for you. Then, when you have time, you can decide which practice to use depending upon the time available. Some practices require as few as three minutes, whereas others might require ten or fifteen minutes.

If you are interested in practicing a basic form of mindfulness, try following these simple steps:

1. Set aside some time in a quiet and calming environment. You don't need any special equipment, but it is best if you can sit or lay somewhere that you feel comfortable. It doesn't matter if this is on a bed, in a chair, on a cushion, or even sitting on the floor. Simply, find someplace where you can focus on yourself rather than sitting in an uncomfortable position or outside distractions.

2. Allow yourself to focus on the present moment. You don't have to worry about keeping your mind empty or finding a deep state of inner calm. All you have to do is focus on the present moment without judgment. This may be difficult at first, but with a little practice, you will be able to complete this easily. Don't let any difficulties deter you, as this is a simple form of mindfulness and only requires a little practice.

3. It is normal for judgments to occur while you are focusing on the present. These judgments can be caused by your inner critic, or they may be focused on an outside source. Either way, make a mental note of the judgments, and then let them go and melt away.

4. Your mind might get carried away by thoughts of the future, past, worries, or tasks you must complete. This is okay and a normal part of mindfulness, as your mind will naturally wander. When this happens, you

simply bring your mind back to the present moment to remain focused. The practice of mindfulness is simply bringing your focus back time and again to the present.

5. When your mind wanders be kind to yourself. Don't judge your thoughts or the fact that your mind has wandered. Simply recognize that your thoughts have wandered, and then come back to the present.

6. You can practice this either normally, as stated here, or you can include some deep breathing exercises, as well. You will find that with the addition of deep breathing you can achieve an even greater state of calmness and more easily pull yourself back to the present after your mind has wandered. Now that you understand the most basic mindfulness practice let's explore other forms of mindfulness therapy that you might utilize. Some of these vary in difficulty, but if you

slowly work into it, you will find it becomes easier.

Deep Breathing

There are many benefits of including deep breathing into your mindfulness practices. This exercise has been shown to help lower blood pressure, reduce stress, and decrease heart rate. While stressful situations often trigger the body's fight or flight response, deep breathing is able to calm the sympathetic nervous system, lower adrenaline, and return the body back to its normal state. This is helpful, because while the fight or flight response is needed in times of danger when we are safe but stressed it causes strain on the body. This is because the fight or flight response cannot tell the difference between true danger and stressful stations. Therefore, if you are someone who struggles with stress or the fight or flight response regularly, then you will find that this method can greatly help return you to baseline. With deep breathing you can activate the body's natural relaxation response, promoting healing and a profoundly calm state. Two forms of deep breathing include belly breathing and the four-seven-eight method. First, begin with belly breathing, and after you are adjusted to this you can move on to the following method, which is a little more difficult.

Belly Breathing:

1. Sit or lie down someone in a comfortable and relaxed position.

2. While sitting or laying place one hand on your belly below your ribs. The other hand should be placed on your chest by your heart.

3. Breathe deeply through your nose, allowing your belly to push your hand out in the process. You should be breathing from your belly, meaning that the hand on your chest should not move during the breaths.

4. When you breathe out, do it through pursed lips, as though you were whistling. Feeling your hand on your belly allow it to sink in as you breathe out. Use the hand on your stomach to help push all of the air out of your lungs.

5. Follow this pattern of deep breathing three to ten times, taking it slowly with every breath.

6. After you finish the exercise examine how you feel and notice any improvements.

Four-Seven-Eight Breathing:

1. Sit or lay down somewhere comfortable. Using the belly breathing method, place one hand on your belly and the other on your chest.

2. Taking a deep breath from your belly through your nose silently count to the number four.

3. After breathing in, count to the number seven while holding your breath.

4. After holding your breath breathe out completely while counting to the number eight. By the time you finish counting you should try to have all of the air out of your lungs.

5. Repeat this process three to seven times, until you feel a deep state of calmness.

6. Notice how you are feeling after completing the exercise and take note of any improvements.

Body Scan

The body scan method of mindfulness is a wonderful way to relax and calm your mind. However, it is about more than just being calm. Rather, this practice requires a person to become aware of the different regions of their body. During this process, you become attuned to how each portion of your body feels, without trying to change it. You are simply present and aware. This allows you to get in touch with your body, release the daily stress of needing to accomplish tasks, and let go of pent-up emotions. This form of mindfulness, like others, also promotes a state of focus. By switching your focus between the different regions of your body you are training your mind to be able to focus on different factors on command more easily.

You begin the body scan practice by laying flat on your back with your arms next to you and palms facing upward. Your legs should be relaxed with your feet slightly apart. While this method is ideally done while laying down, feel free also to try doing it while sitting in a comfortable chair. If you choose to do this exercise sitting, then ensure that your feet are resting solidly on the floor and that your palms are facing upward.

Whether sitting or standing, be sure to stay as still as possible during the entire duration of the exercise. If you must move at one point, then move delivery while remaining aware of how it feels, your position, and remain in a deeply calm state. After you are comfortable to become aware of your breathing, notice its rhythm and how it feels while it comes in and out of your lungs. As it enters and exits your nostril, experience how it feels to take air in and then fully expel it. While you want to become aware of your breathing, don't try to change it. During this time you aren't practicing deep breathing exercises or trying to alter how you usually breathe. Simply breathe in your normal way while remaining completely focused and aware of it. Once you are fully aware of your breathing, move onto how your body feels. You want to notice your temperature against that of the environment, the texture of the cloth against your skin, the pressure of what you are sitting or laying on against your body. If any areas of your body are sore, tingling, or feel either light or heavy bring them to your attention. Note any areas of your body that are feeling hypersensitive of lack sensation.

After you have created a general state of awareness of your body begin to note every area of your body down from your toes up to your head. You always want to start from the lower portions of the body and then move upward.

A typical body scan includes focusing on these body parts in order:

- Toes
- Feet and ankles
- Calves
- Knees
- Thighs
- Pelvic area
- Abdomen
- Chest
- Lower back
- Upper back

- Fingers

- Hands and wrists

- Arms

- Neck

- Face and head

Once you have completed your body scan for five to seven minutes, note how you feel, both physically and mentally. By understanding how this practice helps you, then you will better know when to utilize it in the future.

Create a Safe Place

When beginning this exercise, you first want to create a sense of calmness and peace deep within. You can do this by sitting in a quiet and comfortable location. Close your eyes and simply focus on your breathing for one or two minutes. You don't have to practice deep breathing; you simply want to be aware of your breathing and focus on nothing else. Once you have focused on your breathing for a minute or two expand your focus so that you are feeling the sensations of your entire body. You want to practice this for about a minute until you find yourself in a state of deep calmness.

Feel that deep calmness? Once you find that peace and safety remain with your eyes closed, but imagine looking around yourself. What do you see when you look around with your mind's eye? Imagine a calm and peaceful place, anywhere that you feel most comfortable. This location may be a meadow with a brook, a forest with tall trees and damp leaves, an abandoned castle in the middle of a forest filled with old books and plants, a calm beach at sunset, or even your grandparent's house that you would visit on holiday.

Wherever your calm place is, focus on what you can see and feel there. Do you feel the sun on your skin? The breeze gently blowing your hair? Water from the side brushing back and forth on your feet? The warmth of fire against your face? The spines of worn ancient books against your fingertips? The warmth of the oven warming your entire body? Focus on the environment and notice everything that you can feel in this safe place.

After you create a strong connection of what you can feel, focus on what you can hear. Do you hear birds calling? Ocean waves crashing against the shore? Fire crackling as it burns the wood? A hand beater mixing cake batter? Book pages turning? Animals in the distance calling to each other? Soft music? Next, focus on the sense of smell. Do you smell the salty waves of the ocean? Fresh pine and jasmine? Dusty books? Smoke from the bonfire? Vanilla or chocolate cake as it cooks in the oven? The musty scent of a large cat?

Allow your entire body to relax as you imagine yourself in this safe space. Let the muscles in your neck, shoulders, and face go limp. Relax your arms and legs. Feel free to smile as you enjoy being surrounded in your safe space. Lastly, imagine that not only do you enjoy your safe place but that this place enjoys having you in its presence, as well. When you arrive in this location both you and your safe space experience joy. You and this place share a deep emotional connection. Whenever you are stressed or need to feel at peace, love, or safe, you can come to this place to experience rejuvenation.

The Compassionate State

You will find that completing this exercise can help you develop a better sense of self. This exercise will also help you to develop more compassion over time, which you can then use on yourself and those around you.

To begin this exercise, once again create a peaceful and calm state. To do this sit or lay somewhere comfortable and focus on your natural breathing. Don't worry about deep breathing exercise or altering your breathing. You simply want to focus on how you naturally breathe.

After your body and mind have calmed and become focused, you can begin the exercise. Begin by imagining yourself as a compassionate person, who can feel, think, and act in a compassionate manner. Think of the qualities of compassion, such as warmth, wisdom, strength, and responsibility. Fantasize that you possess these qualities. First, imagine that you have these qualities starting with wisdom. This deep sense of wisdom originates from a fundamental understanding of the mind, body, and nature of life.

Next, after you fully feel the quality of wisdom begin to imagine that you have a compassionate strength. Imagine that you have the strength to understand not only your own struggles but the struggles of others, as well. In a non-judgmental way, you can be tolerant, sensitive, and withstand struggles. Allow your body to naturally change postures in a way that reflects this compassionate strength.

After you understand wisdom and strength focus on feeling the element of warmth. Imagine that you show warmth and kindness to both yourself and others. Feel that you can reach out to others with warmth, imagining what it must feel like. Envision yourself talking to someone with warmth and kindness, noticing the tone of voice you use while completing this exercise using an expression that portrays this warmth.

Lastly, visualize that you have a strong sense of responsibility. You have no interest in blaming, judging, or condemning others or yourself; you simply wish to help everyone through their difficult circumstances. Remember to hold onto your warmth, strength, and wisdom. Fully commit yourself to be wholly compassionate.

You may not possess all of these qualities at this time. You may not be a very compassionate person. That's okay. If you visualize yourself having these qualities and work towards gaining them, then you will slowly grow into them. Nobody will become passionate overnight, you simply have to keep working toward your goal and you will get there. Being wise, strong, responsible, and warm takes practice, as does everything else.

Flowing Compassion

Sit or lay somewhere quiet and calm, where you know that you won't be disturbed. Focus on calm natural breathing until you are relaxed. Then, think back to a time when you are compassionate, kind, and caring to either another human or an animal. Although, try to think of a situation in which the animal or human was happy. You do not want a situation in which they were distressed, as you might begin to focus on the stress of the situation rather than the compassion. While visualizing the situation, focus on the feelings of kindness and warmth, on your desire to help the other human or animal. Your focus shouldn't be how the animal or human responses to your compassion, but rather your intentions of kindness. Visualize yourself slowly growing as you imagine the compassion you were expressing. Imagine growing wiser, stronger, warmer, calmer, and more responsible, able to help the other person or animal better.

Focus on your body; remember the experience of how it feels to be kind and compassionate. Allow the warmth to flow through your body while you notice the genuine compassion and well-wishes for the person or animal to fully flourish. Consider the kind and compassionate words you might say your tone of voice, and actions you took to help. Visualize how nice it felt to be compassionate. Lastly, focus completely on your desire to be compassionate, helpful, and kind. Notice the feeling of expansion, the flow of warmth, with wise words and actions, the kind tone of voice. After you finish focusing on this, you may consider taking notes on how it felt.

By using this exercise, you will find that you increase your desire to be compassionate, as well as your knowledge in how to act on this desire. As you continue to practice this exercise, your compassion will slowly increase, and you will become better at directing your compassion both inward and outward.

Focusing Compassion Inward

You have both an anxious self and a troubled self. You can use this inner compassion mindfulness technique to help direct compassion inward. But, while you can direct the compassion to both of these selves, you can only do one at a time. Therefore, if you wish to direct compassion toward both selves, you will have to follow through with the exercise twice, focusing on one of the selves in turn. In order to use this technique, it will help if you have first learned how to use the previously mentioned Compassionate State technique, in which you visualize yourself as being full of compassion.

The Troubled Self:

Firstly, you will want to sit or lay down in a quiet and peaceful area. Close your eyes and notice the feeling of your body. Focus on reaching the compassionate state as mentioned previously, ensuring that your facial expression is one conveying warmth. Envision that you are outside of yourself, watching your actions as though you were watching someone else or a recording. Imagine watching yourself waking up and getting out of bed in the morning, moving around the house, and preparing for a usual day. As you watch this "recording" of yourself remember to feel compassion and kindness toward you that you are watching. Notice the self-critical and troubling thoughts and emotions you in the recording are expressing. Pay attention to their struggle with compassion without letting it weight or bog you down. Continue watching with your compassionate self with the intention of sharing warmth, kindness, strength, wisdom, and aid.

If your compassionate self begins to fade away then release the "recording" of yourself and go back to the compassionate state exercise. Regain your sense of peace and compassion. Find your gentle expression full of warmth. Then, after you regain this, you may go back to the recording and watching yourself

By completing this exercise regularly, you can find a more objective and compassionate view of yourself. You will be able to see your struggles, the difficult things you go through, and appreciate yourself for them. Through completing this exercise, you can become more intuitive and accepting of yourself.

The Anxious Self:

Whether you have been diagnosed with an anxiety disorder or simply struggle with anxiety at points in your life, this version of the technique will help you manage and release some anxiety. This is because by finding compassion for your anxious self, you will understand how to manage your anxiety better and are less likely to punish yourself for experiencing it. Spend a few minutes to tap into your compassionate self, as you learned previously. Feel the warm expression on your face, the sense of kindness, wisdom, strength, and responsibility. Focus on this sense of compassion and peace while you breathe normally.

Following, envision yourself in a situation where you are anxious. This may be a past situation or an imagined situation that has not previously occurred. While imagining this stressful situation, remember to maintain your compassionate self.

Move outside of your body and watch yourself as though you were watching a recording. Notice how you become anxious, how you feel and act. Find understanding, compassion, and empathy for this anxious self.

Fantasize about how you would like to help your anxious self and what you might say to them to lessen the anxiety. You may choose to encourage them, recognize their ability to get through the struggle or validate their emotions. Whatever you choose to say, let it come from a place of compassion, kindness, and helpfulness.

As time gradually moves in this vision, see the anxiety slowly reducing and lessening until it is completely gone. Experience how it feels to come through the situation and offer your anxious self some understanding, encouragement, and kindness. Express to them the courage they showed by getting through the period of anxiety.

Later on, whenever you are in a situation that causes an increase in anxiety, practice using deep or rhythmic breathing. Slow down and remind yourself of the compassionate self. See yourself through these eyes and acknowledge the struggle you are going through. Encourage and be kind to yourself.

As you can see, there are many types of medication and mindfulness. In this book, we have only been able to touch on a small number of the techniques, but if you use them regularly, you will soon experience many great benefits.

Chapter 9: Helpful Questions for Unhelpful Thoughts

Automatic thoughts are thoughts that occur quickly throughout our daily lives. Oftentimes, we are not even aware of these automatic thoughts as they pass as quickly as they occur. All the same, these thoughts can cause damage to our psyche, as they are often negative in nature. The thoughts may be negativity directed at ourselves, such as "I'm a failure," or it could be directed at another person, such as "they are so annoying, they don't even care!" Either way, these automatic thoughts will cause a person to trust and like themselves less, and decrease their compassion toward other people.

Thankfully, even if you have negative or skewed automatic thoughts, there is something you can do about it. Largely, with the help of cognitive restructuring.

We have mentioned cognitive restructuring in previous chapters, which is a therapeutic practice which helps people challenge and replaces their irrational or negative thoughts. However, in this chapter, you will learn in more detail how to use cognitive restructuring to replace unhelpful thoughts with helpful questions.

One well-established way to practice cognitive restructuring is with Socratic questioning. While cognitive distortions can be pervasive and damaging, with Socratic questioning, you can find, identify, challenge, and replace negative and false ideas. In the place of these negative ideas, you can find truthful, helpful, and positive thoughts.

The first step in replacing these false and damaging thoughts is to find and identify them. You can do this by increasing your awareness of your thoughts, especially those of a negative nature. Don't get discouraged if this takes time. It is natural for it to take time to become more aware of ourselves and our thoughts. It is unlikely that you have experience stopping yourself in the intense middle emotions to question what thoughts triggered the emotions. But, this is what is needed to practice inner awareness. It may be difficult at first, but it is by far worth the effort, and over time it will become easier.

During the beginning it is often too difficult to immediately jump into a situation that is emotionally volatile, only to stop and analyze your emotions. Therefore, consider behaviors that you wish to stop or change, and then identify what triggers these behaviors. Then, in the future, whenever you are in one of these situations you can be more aware that you are experiencing cognitive distortions.

For instance, you might start to experience anxiety, sweating, and accelerated heart rate before going to a party. Maybe, when you have a large project to accomplish you put it off in favor of smaller projects.

When you are alone in the evenings, perhaps you begin to feel overwhelmingly lonely until you are unable to manage. Or, maybe you find that whenever you have an upcoming stressful event you always start arguments and yelling at the people around you.

Consider these situations. Do you have similar circumstances in your own life that frequently cause you to lash out or experience strong negative emotions? Can you think of any situations that tend to have a larger impact on your mood?

Try your best to find and identify situations that can be triggers or alarms. While it's okay for these situations to be vague, it is better if you can make them as specific as possible. Write out a list of the most significant and commonplace triggers that you experience. You can use this list when working on cognitive restructuring.

Next, when you find yourself in one of these emotional circumstances, work on challenging negative, harmful, irrational, or illogical thoughts with Socratic questioning. Try out some of the following questions to work through the situation, emotions, and thoughts.

- Is this thought process realistic?

- Are these thoughts based on feelings or facts?

- What evidence supports this thought?

- Might I be misinterpreting evidence?

- Am I looking at the situation with a black and white view?

- Is this thought a habit, or are there facts which support it?

Using these questions in your Socratic questioning can be a great start. Try to memorize a few basic questions so that you can always use them. However, if you need more in-depth questioning to help you confront the thoughts and reconstruct your cognition, you might try this full list:

1. Am I believing a thought to be a fact?
2. Am I jumping to conclusions?
3. Am I believing my view must be the only possible view?
4. What are my goals, and will this line of thinking help me achieve them or get in the way?
5. What are the advantages and disadvantages of this thought pattern?
6. Are my thoughts centered on all-or-nothing principles?
7. Are my thoughts using ultimatum-type words?
8. Am I determining my entire worth and value on a single event?
9. Am I focusing only on my weaknesses while forgetting my strengths?
10. Am I blaming myself for something that I am not at fault for?
11. Am I expecting perfection?
12. Am I taking something personally, even if it has little to nothing to do with me?
13. Am I using double standards in my thinking?

14. Am I overestimating the likelihood of a disaster?

15. Am I only paying attention to the negative and ignoring the positive?

16. Am I exaggerating the importance of something?

17. Are my thoughts predicting the future rather than testing it?

18. Am I focusing on and worrying about how things should be rather than how they actually are?

19. Am I assuming I'm unable to change my situation?

When using these questions, you first need to identify a specific thought that you wish to confront. This thought should be one that you believe is causing you harm, anxiety, pain, or which might be irrational. You want to target thoughts which you find yourself frequently struggling with especially.

After you have a thought, use these questions to consider if the thought has any evidence supporting it. What evidence supports it and which evidence negates it? Knowing this will help you determine the truth of the thought. Once you have evidence both for and against the thought weigh it out and determine which one is more likely, is the thought true or false? This can help you determine if the thought originates from facts, or if it has been created by your feelings.

Once you determine whether a question is true or false, you can determine if the situation is truly black and white. There are usually many shades of gray in a situation, but our cognitive distortions can cause us to see them as black and white. Oftentimes, situations are much more complex than we consider.

Consider, might other people view and interpret the situation differently than you? If they are, how do you think they might interpret it? Think, is your interpretation truly the only way to view the situation, or are there any other valid interpretations, as well? When compared to other interpretations does yours still seem likely?

Next, analyze whether or not you are looking at all of the needed evidence, or if you are only looking at the evidence you wish to see. People will often only wish to see the evidence which backs up what they already believe, as they don't wish to be contradicted. Try to remain objective.

Sometimes, our negative thoughts are based in truth, but they are still not completely true. This is because they are an exaggeration of the truth, a warped truth. Consider if your thought might be an exaggerated truth or not.

After you have analyzed the evidence supporting and contradicting a thought, consider how you came to have this thought. Did someone pass this thought onto you? If so, is this person someone you can reliably trust to tell you the truth in this situation?

Finally, after you have completely analyzed the situation and thoughts, consider how likely the thought is to be true or false. What backs this thought up? What contradicts this thought? Is your thought likely, or is it an unlikely worst-case scenario? Try to consider the situation rationally, calmly, and objectively.

This Socratic questioning process encourages you to look deep inside yourself. To consider what thoughts you struggle with and whether or not they are true. If your thoughts are not coming from a place of truth, then you can learn and more easily release them to replace with something more reasonable and healthy.

You may also try keeping a thought record to help you analyze your thoughts. This record is written down on paper, which will help you to better question your thoughts, better analyze the situation, and increase the likelihood of you adopting a new and healthier thought process. Thought records are a common practice and tool used in cognitive behavioral therapy. The records can help us to more easily challenge thoughts that would usually go unquestioned. While there are different ways in which you can structure a thought record, they generally include sections in which you can journal your thoughts, situation, feelings, behaviors, and new alternative thoughts.

Once you have completed a thought record, you will find that you have a more balanced and truthful alternative view from the original. But, not only is the end result helpful, the process of filling out a thought record in itself is a helpful practice. This is because, as you fill out your thought record you begin to notice your inner self better and come to understand your own feelings, thoughts, and motives better. While we are often out of touch with our inner selves, by filling out a thought record you are forced to pay attention to this inner self and come to a better understanding. This process often creates its own shift in your emotions and feelings. The benefits can continue down the road, as well, as you develop a habit of looking inward at yourself. Following you will find an example of a thought record, which you can use in your own life. Try to fill it out in a notebook, but you can certainly alternatively store the record on your phone.

Situation:
When and where did the situation happen?
Where other people involved?
What exactly happened?

Mood:
Afraid
Anxious
Depressed
Guilty
Angry

Automatic Thoughts/Images:
"I'm an idiot."
"Nobody likes me."
"I'll never improve."
"Nobody will ever date/marry me."
"I'll never get a good job."
"I'll fail my test."

Evidence that Supports the Thoughts:
I made a mistake.
My friend didn't call me back.

I'm not good at math.

My significant other dumped me.

Evidence that Does Not Support the Thoughts:

I answer more questions correctly than I get wrong.

I have improved on my practice tests.

I have friends who contact me when they have the time.

I can see I have already improved

Balanced Alternative Thoughts:

"I may not be good at all subjects, but I am intelligent."

"I have multiple friends who show me love."

"I am already improving, and I will continue to improve."

"People have dated me in the past, and I'll find the right person someday."

If you find that your thoughts are largely true, don't despair. In this case, you can come up with a plan to confront and address the situation. After all, once you are aware of a situation and make a plan, you can finally start making progress. But, if you continue to ignore the thought and let it control you, then you will only stay where you are at. For instance, if you believe you can't get a good grade on a paper, then you can make a plan in order to help you learn and practice to improve.

Next, rate how much you now believe the new thoughts on a scale of zero to one-hundred percent. You will often find that how much you believe in the balanced alternative thought is dependent on your mood.

Lastly, rate your moods, as well. You will want to rate the moods you previously wrote down, as well as any new moods. If you find that your mood hasn't improved, then go through the thought record again and see if there is any place that you can be more thorough, accurate, or specific.

You will find that by consistently writing this information down, you can find thought patterns you wouldn't have previously noticed, consider things in a new light, and find cognitive distortions you were previously unaware of.

Conclusion

Cognitive behavioral therapy may be largely unknown in the general population. But, therapists and people who have used this therapy know full-well the benefits it can provide. You now have an understanding of cognitive behavior therapy and how you can use it to increase your health, improve your anxiety, decrease depression, manage addiction, overcome anger, and stop negative thinking. Not only can you use this therapy with the help of a trained therapist, but you are also able to practice its techniques on your own in the comfort of your home. You have the tools you need to succeed. Yet, remember that the tools of cognitive behavioral therapy are meant to work together, not as sole techniques. Therefore, to reap the many benefits of CBT use a comprehensive approach and utilize the many tools presented in this book. If you are thorough, focused, and consistent you can experience the benefits many have gone through before you.

As you continue to progress through the tools within these pages, you will learn how to replace your negative thoughts with positive, become more aware of your inner self, learn to control your automatic thoughts, and more. The more time and patience you put into using these techniques the more benefits you will experience until you find that your life is flourishing.

Thank you for reading Cognitive Behavioral Therapy! You have nothing to fear going forward. You have all of the tools you need, and I know that you can attain your goals. Whether you are using CBT to help you decrease anxiety, stop anger, manage addiction, control depression, or a number of other issues, you can do it. Many people have come before you and proven that it is possible.

Made in the USA
Middletown, DE
08 November 2019